From Religion to Relationship

Finding Jesus in a Divided Church

Jose Perez, Pastor, Rock of Salvation

Table of Contents

Dedication

To my parents, Reverend Jose Perez and Reverend Ramona Perez, who laid the spiritual foundation I now walk on. Your courage and obedience brought the gospel to New England, and your legacy still shapes my steps, even through seasons of pain and separation.

To my sons, Jose Ramon Cruz and Carlos Miguel Cruz, whose absence has left a permanent ache in my heart, but whose memory fuels my calling to speak life into the broken. You remind me that heaven is real—and that the battle for souls is urgent and worth it.

To my wife, Cheryl Marie, my companion of over 36 years, thank you for staying through every storm, for loving me through every trial, and for standing by my side when the world—and even family—felt far away. You are my earthly strength, my gift from God.

To my children and grandchildren—and to the future generations of our family and church: May this book light the fire of the Spirit in your hearts and awaken you to your true identity in Christ.

And to Rock of Salvation Church, thank you for continuing the mission, not of religion, but of truth, grace, and the Spirit of God alive in us.

This is for every dry bone. Every broken believer. Every soul that still hears the voice of the Lord calling, "Live."

In Loving Memory

This book is lovingly dedicated to the memory of my beloved sons, Jose Ramon Cruz and Carlos Miguel Cruz.

Jose Ramon, my firstborn, whose life was brief but full of light: You taught me how to love deeply, even amid sorrow. Though bacterial meningitis took you at six years old, your memory still beats in every heartbeat of this ministry.

Carlos Miguel, whose life was taken by violence far too soon on May 8, 2021, at the age of 44: You lived boldly, and your passion continues to inspire me. Your loss shook me to the core, yet God's grace continues to carry me through the pain.

You both are with the Lord now, beyond the reach of sickness and sorrow, embraced by perfect peace. Until we meet again, I will preach, teach, and lead with the fire and purpose that your lives helped ignite within me.

This work is also a reflection of the unwavering support of my wife, Cheryl Marie, whose love, strength, and faith have carried me through life's darkest valleys and most sacred callings.

This work is part of your legacy. Your names are written on every page.

With eternal love, Dad

Introduction

These people honor me with their lips, But their heart is far from me; In vain do they worship me, teaching as doctrines the commandments of men.
– Matthew 15:8-9 (ESV)

I was born in Puerto Rico in 1953, and from an early age, I found myself caught between two worlds, torn by the tension of different cultures and the deeper struggle between the religious tradition of my ancestors and the living presence of Jesus Christ. My life has been marked by rebellion, redemption, loss, and restoration—but more than anything, by the relentless grace of God.

This book is not an attack on the Church. It is a cry from the valley of dry bones. I've seen what religion without relationship produces. I've watched the weight of man-made systems crush the very people Jesus came to save. And I've lived it too—walking in pain, failure, and silence until God met me in a supernatural moment that changed everything.

My journey includes addiction, grief, family division, and the deaths of two sons. When my father, a pioneering pastor, passed leadership to me, it fractured our family. Yet even when I was surrounded by darkness, Jesus didn't let go. He called me, not because I was strong, but because He is faithful.

I've come to believe the greatest crisis in the Church today isn't politics or programs—it's that we've forgotten who we're following. We've substituted presence with performance. We've built churches on systems instead of surrender. We've taught commandments of men as if they were the gospel of Christ.

But it's not too late. That's what this book is about. Here, we'll explore the foundation Jesus laid, the example of the apostles, the role of the Holy Spirit, and the practices that return us to intimacy with God. Each chapter includes Scripture, reflection, and a call to action. Transformation doesn't happen through reading alone, but through encounter. Whether you're burned out, broken, or just hungry for more, this is an invitation—not to religion, but to relationship. Jesus is still building His Church, not with bricks or denominations, but with hearts made alive by His Spirit.

Let's take the journey together.

Jose R. Perez

Pastor, Rock of Salvation Church

Worcester, Massachusetts

Part I:

Foundations

Thus says the Lord God to these bones: Behold, I will cause breath to enter you, and you shall live – Ezekiel 37:5 (ESV)

Chapter 1:

The Church Jesus Built vs. the One Man Created

Section 1: Returning to the Cornerstone

I still remember the first Sunday after the church split. The sanctuary was unusually quiet, though the pews still held the warmth of recent gatherings. Where voices once rose in unified praise, only silence lingered—heavy, unsettled. Some sat in their usual places, eyes lowered. Others drifted toward the back, unsure of where they now belonged. The room felt thick, not with the Spirit, but with grief and confusion.

That morning, I stood behind the pulpit, Bible in my trembling hands. My father had entrusted me with the church before his passing. It should have been a sacred honor. Instead, it sparked a storm.

My mother, who had prayed and preached in that sanctuary for decades, believed the mantle should have fallen to her. She left, and many followed—family, longtime members, spiritual sons and daughters. I wasn't just preaching to a smaller crowd; I was facing the fragmented remains of a spiritual body I had grown up in.

Though I knew God had called me, I couldn't shake the feeling that I had failed them all.

A Whisper From the Spirit

That Sunday, as I stood silently at the pulpit, the Spirit whispered words I will never forget: "You are not the cornerstone—I am." That truth pierced the weight I was carrying. I had been trying to hold the church together with perfect sermons, strategic leadership, and sheer willpower. But this was never mine. Not my father's. Not my mother's. If the church wasn't built on Jesus, it would never stand. Peter said it plainly in Acts 4:11: "This Jesus is the stone that was rejected by you, the builders, which has become the cornerstone."

That verse hits differently when you've witnessed rejection firsthand—not of doctrine, but of Christ's Spirit. When leaders trade humility for hierarchy, and churches choose control over compassion, the wounds run deep. Jesus was never embraced by religious systems. He didn't seek their permission. While they built temples, He flipped tables. While they fought for titles, He knelt to wash feet. They wanted a Messiah who would reinforce their traditions, but Jesus called them to leave those traditions behind.

Where religion builds walls, Jesus tears them down. *Ephesians 2:14* says He "has broken down in His flesh the dividing wall of hostility." When religion demands control, Jesus offers freedom. He wasn't rejected because He was wrong—He was rejected because He was a threat.

And tragically, we've kept building on that same foundation of pride and performance ever since.

Building on the Wrong Foundation

How many churches today are built more on charisma than on Christ? On branding more than the Bible? We promote pastors like celebrities, count attendance instead of transformation, and pledge loyalty to denominations over devotion to Jesus.

Many who walk away from church today aren't rejecting God. They're rejecting a distorted version of Him—a religion that bears His name but not His heart. A building full of people, yet empty of His Spirit. A pulpit that shouts holiness but barely whispers grace.

And still, Jesus is not intimidated by fractured churches or divided sanctuaries. He is still calling us back—**back to the Cornerstone.**

How the Early Church Got It Right

What I experienced personally, the Church has experienced historically. When the Spirit fell at Pentecost, there were no denominations. No stage lights. No platforms or streaming services. Just broken people, ignited by the Holy Spirit, following Jesus wherever He led.

The early Church had no cathedrals or clout. They met in house churches, shared meals, and showed sacrificial love. They were united—not by uniformity, but by the Spirit. Their boldness came from their belief. Like David before Goliath, they faced danger without armor. Their courage didn't come from institutional approval but from knowing the God who had delivered them before.

Like Daniel in the lions' den, they stood firm when the world tried to silence them. But that unity didn't last. By the time of Constantine, the Church became a tool of empire. Structures replaced Spirit. Creeds replaced relationship. The Church became an institution rather than a movement.

Now, structure itself isn't the enemy. Leadership has its place. But when form replaces fire, and when leaders dominate instead of serve, we lose our way. Jesus didn't die to produce weekly performances. He died to tear the veil, bring us to the Father, and fill us with His Spirit. He called us to heal the broken, proclaim good news to the poor, and set captives free. That calling has not changed. But too often, we've changed the foundation.

The Invitation to Return

That first Sunday after the split could have been the end. Instead, it became a beginning because we laid down our pride and stopped pretending that we had all the answers. We let God be God again.

Healing came slowly—not through programs, but through raw worship, honest preaching, and a simple return to Jesus. People didn't just attend. They connected. And the Spirit breathed life into dry bones once again.

> If your church is fractured...

> If your soul feels distant...

> If your faith has grown cold...

The answer is not a new system. The answer is still Jesus. The stone the builders rejected has become the cornerstone.

This book is for pastors, prodigals, and seekers alike. It's not an invitation to a place—but to a Person. Not the Jesus of branding or politics, but the One who knelt in the dirt, stood before accusers, and still opens His arms wide to the weary and the wandering.

Let's return to the Cornerstone—not in theory, but in practice. In our homes. In our pulpits. In our quiet moments and our loud services. Let every stone we lay in ministry begin with Jesus Himself. Let's rebuild what man has broken. **Let's find Jesus again—not in religion, but in relationship.**

Section 2: Constantine to Denominations—What Went Wrong?

It's difficult to pinpoint exactly when the Church lost its way. The early believers had Jesus, the apostles, the Holy Spirit, and authentic community. So how did we end up here, with tens of thousands of denominations, political infighting, consumer Christianity, and churches that reflect the world more than the Word?

To understand that, we must examine one of the most pivotal turning points in Church history: the moment the cross became entangled with the crown.

A Dangerous Alliance: Constantine and the Empire

In A.D. 313, Emperor Constantine issued the Edict of Milan, granting religious tolerance to Christians throughout the Roman Empire. After centuries of brutal persecution, this appeared to be a miraculous victory. But Jesus never sought the empire's approval, and He certainly never modeled worldly power as a pathway to godliness.

According to legend, Constantine had a vision of a cross with the words, "In this sign, conquer." He wielded the cross as a battle standard—not as a surrender to Christ, but as a tool for dominance. Though baptized only on his deathbed, Constantine's political embrace of Christianity reshaped its entire structure. What had been an underground movement now became an imperial institution.

Like Adam and Eve's decision to eat from the wrong tree, Constantine's influence introduced corruption into what God had created to be pure. The Church gained buildings, wealth, and social clout, but it was all at the cost of simplicity, surrender, and spiritual power.

The rise of imperial Christianity marked a shift from discipleship to dominance, from prayer to politics, from following Jesus to managing religion. Much like Israel clamoring for a king to replace divine leadership, the Church reached for power it was never meant to hold.

Councils, Creeds, and Control

Under Constantine's reign, the Church began organizing large councils to define orthodoxy. The Council of Nicaea in A.D. 325, often celebrated for its theological contributions, also marked the beginning of state-sponsored Christianity. While many doctrines were clarified with good intent, the method was deeply political.

Disagreement no longer led to discussion—it led to exile, excommunication, or even execution.

Bishops became regional governors. Creeds turned into imperial mandates. Dissent was no longer just theological—it was treasonous. Faith became formalized. Church became systematized. And spiritual leadership slowly evolved into religious bureaucracy. Theology became a tool of empire rather than a testimony of grace.

And yet, God was never bound by Rome. While Western Christianity formalized and politicized the faith, God preserved a remnant. Far from the halls of power, the Ethiopian Church safeguarded sacred writings that never passed through Roman councils.

Later discoveries like the Dead Sea Scrolls revealed streams of thought untouched by institutional control, reminding us that the Spirit cannot be confined by kings or councils.

The Church born in the upper room had become a court functionary in Caesar's throne room. And from there, it began to splinter.

From One Body to Many Branches

In A.D. 1054, the Great Schism formally split the Church into Eastern Orthodoxy and Roman Catholicism. This wasn't a theological dispute as much as a power struggle—cultural, political, and geographical.

Then, in 1517, Martin Luther nailed his 95 Theses to a church door in Wittenberg, calling out corruption and igniting the Protestant Reformation. It was an act of bold truth-telling. But instead of unity through repentance, the Church fragmented further.

Lutherans. Baptists. Presbyterians. Methodists. Pentecostals. Non-denominational movements. Today, over 45,000 Christian denominations exist worldwide. Some call this diversity. But many of these divisions didn't arise from deep biblical differences. They stemmed from pride, politics, and personal preference—disputes about baptism style, music selection, spiritual gifts, or even clothing.

We say we're divided over doctrine, but often, we're divided over control. Paul addressed this early when he wrote, "One of you says, 'I follow Paul'; another, 'I follow Apollos'... Is Christ divided?" (1 Corinthians 1:12–13). That question still stings today.

When Doctrine Divides the Body

I've met people cast out of churches for having tattoos, for asking questions, or for being divorced. Jesus didn't reject them, but religion did. The Church was never meant to be a fortress of rank and rules. It was meant to be a Spirit-led family. But over time, we've built altars to tradition and asked God to bless what we've built. And God does not inhabit temples made in our image. He inhabits humble hearts—ones that are open to the Spirit and centered on Christ.

The Personal Cost of Division

When I inherited my father's church—The Rock of Salvation—I carried the weight of legacy. My father, a Borinqueneer and decorated war veteran, had planted that church for our community.

My mother stood beside him, preaching, praying, and leading. When the mantle passed to me, I expected unity. What followed was painful division.

People didn't leave over heresy or scandal. They left over disagreement about who should lead. The split revealed how fragile unity becomes when it's built on personalities rather than Jesus. That experience burned a lesson into my heart: The Church must return to its foundation—not to a brand, a title, or a position, but to Christ alone.

The Witness of Scripture

The Bible is full of stories about restoration after spiritual compromise:

- Moses led a complaining people through a Red Sea they never expected to cross.

- Elijah, isolated and afraid, discovered that God had preserved 7,000 others who had not bowed to Baal.

- David, though morally fallen, was restored to worship and purpose.

- The disciples, who argued over greatness, were still chosen to launch the Church.

- And Ezekiel—standing in a valley of dry bones—was told to prophesy life over death: "O dry bones, hear the word of the Lord... I will cause breath to enter you, and you shall live" (Ezekiel 37:4–5).

If God could restore life to dead bones, He can breathe new life into the divided and disillusioned Church today.

What Now?

We can't undo 1,700 years of institutional religion in a moment. But we can return to Jesus. We can refuse to idolize denominations. We can repent for elevating systems over the Spirit. This is not rebellion. It's restoration. The Church Jesus birthed is still breathing. You'll find it in prison ministries, home fellowships, youth revivals, and whispered prayers at kitchen tables. It's been buried, not erased. Hidden, but not powerless. Waiting—not for the next strategy, but for a fresh surrender.

Let's stop asking God to bless what we've built, and let's start building on what He already blessed: His Word, His Spirit, and His Son. Because the Church isn't a brand or a bureaucracy. It's a Body. His Body. And it's time we live like it again.

A Personal Invitation: Finding Jesus Again in the Word

Even through centuries of compromise and confusion, one thing remains clear: The Bible still reveals Jesus. Despite what Western civilization has done with the Word—twisting it for power, politics, and empire—God's voice still breaks through the pages. If you're willing to push past the noise, the programs, and the traditions of man, you will find Him. I did. At one point, I had to stop listening to what everyone else was saying. I was tired of secondhand sermons, borrowed opinions, and corrupted portrayals. I needed to know who Jesus *really* was—not who I had made Him out to be, and not who the system said He was. So, I opened the New Testament and began to search.

I wasn't reading academically—I was reading to survive. I needed to know Jesus for myself. And there He was—not the Jesus of religion, but the Jesus of redemption. Not the one who fit into neat theological boxes, but the One who broke chains, flipped tables, and loved the unlovable. He wasn't who I expected. He wasn't who I wanted. He was better.

I discovered that you can't truly help someone unless you're willing to dive deep into who they are. That's what I did with Jesus. And the only place I found unfiltered truth about Him was in the Word of God.

One verse especially gripped me—Luke 4:18: "The Spirit of the Lord is upon me, because He has anointed me to proclaim good news to the poor. He has sent me to proclaim liberty to the captives…"

That's the Jesus I found. That's the Jesus still calling us today. This is an individual journey. I took it, and I urge you to do the same. Don't settle for tradition, headlines, or hearsay. Open the Scriptures. Seek Him with all your heart. He's not hiding. He's waiting.

Section 3: Finding the True Church Again

It's a question I've asked more than once—in prayer, in frustration, and in the stillness of an empty sanctuary: **Where is the Church Jesus built?** Not the one on the sign or etched into the bylaws—but the one He said the gates of hell would not overcome (Matthew 16:18). The one born at Pentecost, rooted in the apostles' teaching, empowered by the Spirit, and defined not by structure but by surrender.

I remember one day after a tense leadership meeting. We had spent hours debating property, policies, and power—yet no one had mentioned souls, outreach, or prayer.

As I sat in my office afterward, weary and disheartened, I looked out the window and saw a young woman sitting alone on the church steps. She looked nervous. Worn down. Alone., worn down, and alone.

I stepped outside to meet her. She told me she had passed by the church for weeks but had been too afraid to come in. She had battled addiction. She had lost custody of her daughter. But that day, she said, "Something told me to come find God."

She wasn't looking for a denomination. She was looking for Jesus. The same Jesus who sat with tax collectors, touched the lepers, and wept with the grieving. Her hunger reminded me: The true Church is still alive—but buried under layers of branding, tradition, and human agendas.

Spirit and Truth, Not Brick and Brand

In John 4, a Samaritan woman asked Jesus where the proper place to worship was—Jerusalem or Samaria. We might ask the same today: *Which church is the right one?*

Jesus answered, "The hour is coming, and is now here, when the true worshipers will worship the Father in spirit and truth" (John 4:23). Not in a building. Not by affiliation. Not through style or status. **Spirit and truth.**

The Church Jesus is building doesn't begin with programs—it begins with presence. It's not rooted in platforms or pulpits but in the Spirit moving through surrendered hearts. Where Jesus is truly welcomed, transformation begins. And where the Holy Spirit moves, we find the Church—not always the one we planned, but the one God intended.

Back to the Roots

Acts 2:42 gives us a blueprint for the early Church: "They devoted themselves to the apostles' teaching and the fellowship, to the breaking of bread and the prayers." They didn't have marketing campaigns or ministry consultants.

What they had was:

- **The Word of God**—unfiltered, uncompromised, and alive.

- **Fellowship**—real, Spirit-led relationships, not personality-driven cliques.

- **Breaking bread**—an act of communion and community, remembering Christ's sacrifice and sharing life.

- **Prayer**—not as a transition, but as the Church's breath and lifeline.

And the result? "The Lord added to their number day by day those who were being saved" (Acts 2:47). Miracles happened. Needs were met. Walls fell down. The power of God was not a theory—it was their daily reality.

Today, we have conferences, livestreams, social media strategies, and padded pews—but we often lack the power, unity, and hunger the early Church had. We don't need another ministry calendar. We need a fresh Pentecost.

From Spectacle to Spirit

I'll be honest—I've been caught up in the spectacle. I've worried more about how services looked than whether souls were fed. I've spent more time planning events than prayer meetings.

I've sat in board meetings discussing lighting while people outside sat in spiritual darkness.

But every time I get still before God, I hear Him say the same thing: "Build My Church—not your version of it." That call always leads me back to repentance—not just personal, but corporate.

- We've idolized growth and neglected discipleship.

- We've honored charisma and ignored character.

- We've preached prosperity while avoiding purity.

- We've built followings instead of forming followers.

And the world has noticed. But God is still raising a remnant of believers hungry for more than showmanship. People tired of celebrity Christianity. Churches willing to tear down man-made platforms so the Holy Spirit can move freely again.

The Church Jesus seeks is humble. Holy. Hungry. It makes space for the broken. It holds fast to truth while overflowing with grace. It lifts up Christ—not a brand. It welcomes the prodigal, equips the faithful, and weeps with those who mourn.

You Are the Church

You may be thinking, *"I'm not a pastor. What can I do?"* You can be the Church. You are the temple of the Holy Spirit (1 Corinthians 6:19). A living stone in the house God is building (1 Peter 2:5). You don't need a title. You don't need a microphone.

All you need is a surrendered heart.

- Start a prayer group in your home.

- Disciple someone over coffee.

- Serve your neighbors with compassion.

- Teach your children the Word.

- Invite people not just to church—but into your life.

That's Church. The next move of God isn't waiting on a megachurch—it's waiting on obedience. You may be the spark of revival in your neighborhood, on your block, or right in your own kitchen.

Returning to the Table

One of my favorite resurrection moments is found in Luke 24. Two discouraged disciples were walking the road to Emmaus after Jesus' crucifixion. The risen Christ joined them, but they didn't recognize Him—not on the road, not in conversation, not even in teaching.

They recognized Him at the table. "He took bread and blessed and broke it . . . and their eyes were opened" (Luke 24:30–31). They didn't see Him in the theology. They saw Him in the breaking of bread. That's what we've lost—the table. The place of intimacy. Grace. Real conversation.

The place where family is formed, truth is shared, and masks come off. Jesus is still meeting people there. And maybe that's where He's calling us to return.

It's Time

The true Church was never lost. It's still alive in prison ministries, hospital rooms, home fellowships, and whispered prayers. It's in the voice of a teenager leading worship in a living room. In the hands of a widow laying hold of the promises of God. In the eyes of a former addict who still says, "Jesus, I believe."

This book is not a critique—it's a call. Not to tear down, but to return. Not to blame, but to rebuild. Back to Jesus. Back to the fire. Back to the table. Let's rediscover the Church, letting go of structures and slogans in pursuit of Spirit and truth. **The Church Jesus built is still breathing.**

Let's live like it.

Reflection Questions

Pause and consider these before moving on. Let them guide you closer to Jesus—not just into deeper routine, but into deeper relationship.

1. Are there traditions you've followed without really knowing why?

2. Have you ever felt far from God, even while engaged in religious practices?

3. What might it look like to begin a real relationship with Jesus today?

Remember: Jesus is not asking for habit. He's inviting you into His heart.

Chapter 2:

Apostolic Foundations and Modern Fractions

Section 1: The Traits of the Twelve

The first time I truly reflected on the lives of the twelve apostles, what struck me most wasn't their holiness—it was their humanness. These men weren't spiritual giants when Jesus called them. They were fishermen, tax collectors, skeptics, and zealots. Loud, loyal, doubting, and broken—yet these were the very ones Jesus chose to build His Church.

At a retreat years ago, a young man approached me after I had preached on spiritual leadership. "Pastor," he said, "I don't think I could ever be like Peter or John. They were chosen. They were special."

I looked him in the eye and said, "They weren't special when Jesus found them. They became who they were because they walked with Him."

That truth has never left me. We often think we must be extraordinary to be used by God. But transformation doesn't begin with greatness— it begins with proximity.

Passion, Love, Doubt—They Were Human

Peter was bold, brash, and impulsive—the first to step out of the boat and the first to sink. He declared Jesus the Son of God and then denied Him three times. Yet after Peter's failure, Jesus didn't shame him. He restored him. "Do you love me?" He asked three times. Then came the command: "Feed my sheep." The same Peter who had once crumbled under pressure would later preach with fire at Pentecost. That's grace.

Although John is remembered as the apostle of love, he started as one of the "sons of thunder." At one point, he wanted to call fire down on a Samaritan village. Jesus rebuked him. Yet years later, that same man would write, "God is love." His transformation didn't come from a title. It came from walking closely with the One who is love.

Thomas is often remembered as the doubter. But he was also the one who said, "Let us go, that we may die with Him" (John 11:16). He wasn't rebellious—he was searching. And when he finally said, "Unless I see... I will not believe," Jesus didn't rebuke him. He showed up. He invited Thomas to touch the wounds. He met him in the doubt and offered grace.

There's room for people like Thomas in the Church today. Honest seekers are not a threat—they are a gift.

Transformation by Proximity

The apostles didn't change because they memorized doctrine or climbed a religious ladder. They changed because they walked with Jesus. They sat at His table. They watched Him touch lepers and love outcasts. They saw Him weep, wash feet, and carry the cross. And even after they abandoned Him, He still called them brothers. That kind of love transforms people.

By the time we reach Acts, Peter is preaching with boldness, John is performing miracles, and Thomas is bringing the gospel as far as India. They weren't just improved. They were rebuilt. "They were uneducated, common men... and they recognized they had been with Jesus" (Acts 4:13).

A Snapshot of the Twelve

Their lives remind us: Jesus doesn't call the qualified. He qualifies the called.

Apostle	Strengths	Weaknesses	Legacy
Peter	Passionate, bold	Impulsive, denied Christ	Preached at Pentecost

Apostle	Strengths	Weaknesses	Legacy
James (Zebedee)	Loyal, intense	Harsh temper	First apostle martyred
John	Loving, spiritually deep	Ambitious early on	Wrote Gospel, epistles, and Revelation
Andrew	Humble, invitational	Quiet role	Led others to Jesus
Philip	Logical, sincere	Lacked faith at times	Brought seekers to Jesus
Bartholomew	Honest, devout	Skeptical early on	Early faithful disciple
Matthew	Obedient, generous	Social outcast as tax collector	Gospel author
Thomas	Brave, inquisitive	Needed proof	Declared Jesus as Lord
James (Alphaeus)	Faithful	Little known	Consistent witness
Thaddaeus	Loyal, curious	Spiritually unsure	Asked deep questions
Simon (Zealot)	Zealous, passionate	Possibly extreme	Zeal redirected to Christ
Judas Iscariot	Intelligent, influential	Greedy, betrayed Jesus	Tragic example

The Modern Mirror

When we look at Church leadership today, we don't always see the humility or transformation that marked the apostles. Instead, we often see performers instead of pastors, and legalists instead of lovers of grace.

Some are like Peter before Pentecost—loud and impulsive, eager to lead but slow to listen. Others resemble early John—zealous for purity, but lacking compassion. Some, like Thomas, wrestle with doubt behind theological walls. And yes, there are still some who tragically walk in Judas's footsteps, using Jesus to gain influence and then discarding Him when it no longer suits their goals.

These are sobering, but necessary, truths. If we don't evaluate the kind of leaders we are, and those we choose to follow, we risk repeating the same broken patterns.

Who Are We Following?

I once attended a large Christian conference where the main speaker was treated like a celebrity. There were lights, music, and applause— but no altar call. No space for repentance. No room for the Spirit to move. It felt like a concert. Not a consecrated gathering.

Paul once asked the Corinthians, "Is Christ divided?" (1 Corinthians 1:13). And yet today, we divide over personalities. We defend toxic leaders. We build platforms around charisma instead of character. The apostles weren't forming fan clubs. They were laying the foundation of the Church—a Spirit-filled family rooted in grace and truth.

An Apostolic Invitation

We are not called to admire the apostles. We are called to follow their example. To be like Peter—bold, but surrendered. To be like John— zealous, but shaped by love. To be like Thomas—honest in our doubts and faithful in our pursuit. We are called to walk with Jesus. To be transformed by proximity.

To preach with truth and weep with compassion. To wash feet, carry crosses, and serve without seeking a spotlight. The Church today doesn't need more celebrities. It needs more servants. More shepherds who smell like the sheep. More disciples who bow before they rise. That's the kind of leader I want to be. That's the kind of Church I want to help build. And I believe—Jesus is still calling us to walk that road.

Section 2: The Fall of Spiritual Authority

There's a fine line between spiritual leadership and spiritual control—and many cross it without realizing. Most start with sincere passion: to serve God, preach the truth, and shepherd faithfully. But somewhere along the journey, something shifts. Authority moves from grace to law, from shepherding to ruling. Rules replace relationship. Fear overtakes love. Control erodes compassion.

What began in the Spirit ends up operating in the flesh. We see this clearly in the story of Saul. Before he became Paul—the apostle of grace—Saul embodied religious zeal. He was educated and respected, but also feared. Deadly. He dragged believers from their homes and consented to Stephen's execution. And he did it all believing he was protecting the truth.

But in reality, Saul was persecuting the very people God was trying to save.

From Law to Grace

Saul was a "law leader"—obsessed with control, blind to compassion. And sadly, many pulpits today still echo that same spirit. I remember sitting in a service where the preacher spent 45 minutes condemning clothing, criticizing music, and attacking culture. Jesus wasn't mentioned once. Afterward, a young woman visiting for the first time turned to me and whispered, "I thought God wanted a relationship with me. But now I just feel ashamed." That broke me. When we mix law with grace, we add burdens instead of lifting them. We preach rules instead of redemption. And instead of drawing people to Jesus, we push them away.

Paul later warned the Galatians not to return to legalism after receiving the gospel by faith: "You foolish Galatians! Who has bewitched you?" (Galatians 3:1). Yet two thousand years later, many are still bewitched by control.

A Long Drift From Christ

The Church didn't lose its way overnight. It drifted, slowly and subtly, through pride, compromise, and fear. To trace that drift, we must study our history—not to shame it, but to learn from it.

Date	Event	Effect on the Church
313 AD	Edict of Milan	Christianity legalized, merged with empire
325 AD	Council of Nicaea	Doctrine centralized, Spirit diminished
1054 AD	The Great Schism	Church split into East and West
1517 AD	Martin Luther's 95 Theses	Protestant Reformation begins
1600s	Rise of Baptists and Puritans	Emphasis on personal conviction and Scripture
1700s	Wesleyan Revival	Holiness and methodical discipleship
1906	Azusa Street Revival	Pentecostal fire rekindled
2000s–2020s	Mega-church era	Celebrity culture, hunger, and deconstruction

Each era brought opportunity, and with it, compromise. Somewhere along the way, we traded the upper room for boardrooms. And something sacred was lost.

Why Law Feels Safer

Legalism feels secure because it gives leaders metrics, boundaries, and control. If someone dresses right, speaks right, and follows the rules, they're "in." But grace? Grace is messy. It demands humility, patience, and trust. You can't control grace. You have to live it.

That's why many leaders build fences instead of forming disciples. They discipline before they disciple. They replace the Spirit with structure, and the fruit of the Spirit is exchanged for appearances.

I've seen it happen. People are judged for their clothes while leaders hide secret sins. Congregants are punished for their past while those in power avoid accountability. People walk away—not from Jesus, but from those who misrepresented Him.

Jasmin's Story

A woman in our church—let's call her Jasmin—once shared a heartbreaking story. Years ago, she rushed from work to attend a midweek service. She was wearing pants, and the pastor rebuked her publicly from the pulpit. She left in tears, vowing never to return to church again.

Years later, she walked into our church trembling. I welcomed her. I listened. I reminded her of the woman at the well. Jesus didn't shame her—He sat with her. That's what true spiritual authority looks like. Not condemnation, but compassion.

The Fruit of False Authority

When leadership falls into legalism, the results are devastating. Churches grow cold. Love is replaced by fear. Leaders become gatekeepers instead of shepherds.

And congregants become more loyal to tradition than to truth. Many walk away quietly, labeled "rebellious" or "unsubmissive." But the truth is simpler: They were looking for Jesus and couldn't find Him in the house that bore His name. False teaching doesn't always sound like heresy. Sometimes it sounds like repetition. Sometimes it hides behind rules dressed as righteousness.

Paul warned Timothy: "The time will come when people will not endure sound doctrine... but will gather teachers to suit their own passions" (2 Timothy 4:3). But the danger works both ways. Many flee churches not because they reject truth—but because the truth was never rightly preached within those walls. What they heard was culture, not Christ.

Restoring True Authority

So, how do we restore what's been lost? It starts with repentance.

To pastors, bishops, and leaders: If your leadership has wounded instead of healed, or ruled instead of served, know this: God is not impressed with your title. He's looking at your posture. Repentance doesn't always mean stepping down. But it always means stepping back—from pride, from ego, from control—and returning to the feet of Jesus.

To the wounded: I'm sorry. I'm sorry for every sermon that shamed you. For every leader who misrepresented Christ. For every moment you felt small in the very place you came to feel whole. That wasn't Jesus. That was a broken person pretending to be whole.

But Jesus is still calling you. He still heals. There is still a Church worth belonging to. There is still a Savior who knows your pain.

Let Grace Lead Again

Paul, the former persecutor, became the apostle of grace. If that doesn't prove that no one is too far gone, I don't know what does. But grace doesn't excuse sin—it transforms the sinner. Grace doesn't lower the standard—it raises the heart.

When grace leads, the Church breathes again. The Spirit flows freely. Worship is real. Lives are changed. Let's preach like Paul. Let's lead like Jesus. Let's love like the apostles. Let's rebuild churches rooted in grace, humility, and truth—not fear or performance. Because the Church isn't dying. It's groaning. Groaning for restoration. Groaning for spiritual fathers and mothers. Groaning for leaders who don't lord over but lift. Let's be those leaders. Let's fall to our knees… so we can rise again in Christ.

Section 3: Healing the Divide

The Church doesn't fracture overnight. Division begins small, with a lingering offense, an unresolved disagreement, a slow drift from humility toward ego. A leader pulls away, or a member stops showing up. Trust cracks. Sides form. And before long, the name of Jesus is overshadowed by the noise of disputes. We've seen this pattern unfold throughout history and within our own congregations. But where division grows, grace can still heal.

Denominations and Apostolic Shadows

The Reformation gave us many gifts: Luther's bold stand on grace, Calvin's theological rigor, Wesley's passionate holiness, and Seymour's Pentecostal fire. Yet even the greatest movements of God left behind shadows, where systems calcified into legalism, pride, or personality-driven control.

Some leaders mirrored the apostles—Paul's doctrine, John's love, and Peter's courage. Others—like Constantine or Joseph Smith—introduced teachings and traditions that pulled away from the heart of the gospel. Each of these figures shaped the modern Church, for better or worse. But this isn't just history. Division is deeply personal.

When Grace Is the Answer

Years ago, after a painful leadership conflict, I sat alone in the back pew of our sanctuary. The stained glass scattered afternoon light across empty seats. Moments earlier, a meeting had ended in accusations. Trusted friends now felt like strangers. Some had already left, while others stayed but distanced themselves behind tight smiles.

I prayed, "God, how do we fix this?" He answered with one word: **Grace.**

Peter and Judas: Two Failures, Two Endings

Both Peter and Judas failed Jesus. Both were chosen. Both walked with Him. One betrayed with a kiss; the other denied with a curse. But only one returned. Judas, full of remorse, retreated into shame—and ended his story before grace could reach him.

Peter, also broken, stayed within reach. And Jesus found him. Not to punish, but to restore: "Do you love me?" Peter's failure didn't disqualify him—it refined him. And from that encounter with mercy, he stood and preached at Pentecost. That's what grace does. It doesn't ignore sin. It transforms the sinner.

When Leaders Fall

Leadership failure is one of the deepest wounds a church can face. Some congregations respond with harsh judgment. Others cover it in silence. Both delay healing.

A godly response begins with honesty. Say what's broken. Name what's hurting. Then follow with compassion, not to cover it up but to show care. Leaders, after all, are human. They carry burdens we don't always see. When they fall, we must ask: Are we acting like the crowd that fled—or like Christ, who stayed?

I once sat with a pastor who had lost everything: ministry, reputation, and family. He wept openly. I said, "If Peter could preach again, so can you." Restoration takes time. Repentance. Accountability. But most of all—hope. Church hurt often begins with failure.

But it deepens when the people of grace forget how to extend it.

Personality or Presence?

One of the greatest dangers in today's Church is our worship of personalities. We say we follow Jesus. But often, we build our faith around charisma or branding. And when those personalities fall, everything crumbles. That's what happens when we build on sand.

Jesus warned us: Only houses built on the Rock can withstand the storm (Matthew 7:24–27). If your church collapses when the leader steps down, it wasn't built on Christ. If your faith crumbles when a preacher fails, maybe your eyes were on them—not Him.

We must return to Jesus—not just in word, but in foundation.

My Own Story of Division

When my father passed the mantle of leadership to me, the division was swift. My mother, a deeply respected woman of God, believed the call was hers.

Her departure split not only our church but our family.

Some of my siblings haven't spoken to me since. But through that pain, I've learned something sacred: God still moves in the fracture. He still speaks when the room is empty. He still heals when the heart is breaking.

Healing doesn't always come through reconciliation. Sometimes, it looks like preaching to 10 when you used to preach to 100. Other times, it's praying for those who won't return your calls. Or staying when others walk away.

That's how walls come down. One act of grace at a time.

Two Kingdoms at Work

Behind every division, and beneath every conflict, two spiritual kingdoms are at war:

Kingdom of God	Kingdom of Satan
Spirit of truth	Spirit of deception
Built on Christ	Built on pride
Leads to life	Leads to death
Promotes unity	Promotes division
Operates in light	Operates in darkness
Rooted in grace	Driven by control

"You will recognize them by their fruits" (Matthew 7:16). The test isn't the name on the door—it's the fruit on the tree.

The Church Jesus Is Still Building

Jesus told Peter, "On this rock I will build my church, and the gates of hell shall not prevail against it" (Matthew 16:18). That rock wasn't Peter's gifting—it was his confession: You are the Christ.

That's still the foundation. Not denominations. Not celebrity culture. Not even good theology without Jesus at the center. If we want to heal the Church, we must return to that Rock. Tear down the altars to personalities.

Build again on Christ.

From Pre-Pentecost to Power

The apostles didn't begin as world-changers. Before Pentecost, they were fearful, proud, and uncertain. But Jesus didn't discard them. He transformed them.

A legalist can become a Paul. A denier can become a preacher. A skeptic can become a worshiper. Even a betrayer can repent. But only if we return to Jesus.

Let the Church Rise Again

Healing the divide doesn't begin with strategies. It begins with surrender. The Church Jesus is building is made of forgiven people who are rooted in truth, walking in grace, and refusing to give up on one another. Let that Church rise again. Let that Church be us.

Reflection Questions

Take a moment to reflect on how God sees leadership—and how He sees you.

1. What does it say to you that Jesus chose imperfect people to lead?

2. Have you ever experienced leadership that hurt more than helped?

3. What kind of spiritual leader is God calling you to become?

Remember: God uses the humble—not the perfect—to build His Church.

Chapter 3:

From Dry Bones to Spirit-Filled Life

Section 1: A Valley Full of Bones

In the middle of a vision, between heaven's whisper and earth's groaning, the prophet Ezekiel found himself standing in a valley full of dry bones. Not bodies. Bones. Scattered. Stripped. Lifeless.

The Spirit of the Lord led him there, not to preach, but to see. God wanted Ezekiel to witness what spiritual death looks like when it takes root among His people. This vision wasn't only for Israel back then.

It still speaks to us now.

When Churches Look Alive... but Are Not

Israel had once walked in covenant strength, anchored in the promises given to Abraham, Isaac, and Jacob. But in Ezekiel's day, those promises felt distant. Jerusalem was in ruins. The temple had been destroyed. The people were exiled and broken. Hope had dried up.

Ezekiel stood in that valley surrounded by the remains of something that used to live. And in many ways, that's where much of the Church finds itself today, standing among the remnants of what once was vibrant and alive.

What Ezekiel saw wasn't merely physical—it was prophetic. A mirror of God's people: dry, disconnected, and dying from within.

Today, many churches are busy on the surface but barren in the Spirit. We've traded Pentecost fire for performance lighting. We've substituted revival with routine.

Here's a sobering contrast:

Dry Bones	Spirit-Filled Life
Scattered and powerless	United in Christ
Spiritually dead	Alive in the Spirit
Without purpose	Walking in divine calling
Victims of the past	Healed and restored
Barren	Bearing fruit
Hopeless	Anchored in God's promises
Silent	Speaking life and truth

Revival doesn't begin with noise—**it begins with breath.** The Holy Spirit doesn't come to produce a show. **He comes to bring life.**

National Crisis, Spiritual Collapse

When God asked Ezekiel, "Can these bones live?" The prophet didn't answer with confidence. He said, "O Lord God, You know." That's the voice of someone who has seen too much pain to presume, But still trusts enough to hope.

Israel's exile wasn't merely political—it was deeply spiritual. The prophets had been silenced. Idols were worshiped. Leaders were corrupt. In the midst of that collapse, God gave a vision—not to grieve the past, but to awaken a future.

We may not call it Babylon today, but the symptoms remain familiar:

- Churches that lack power

- Worship that feels mechanical

- Leaders who proclaim performance over presence

- Congregations full of motion but void of breath

We are living in a version of that valley. And the question still remains: **Can these bones live?**

When the Bones Reflect Us

These bones weren't just dead—they were *"very dry."* Scorched by time. Forgotten. Ancient. That's how some of us feel. We pay the bills. We attend services. We raise families. But inside, we're tired. Numb. Disconnected. We sing the songs and quote the Scriptures, but the flames no longer burn. Our faith still believes, but it barely breathes.

I've been there. As a pastor, I've preached sermons I no longer felt. I've encouraged others while silently doubting my own call. I've led with a smile while feeling spiritually hollow. Ministry had become mechanical. The Scriptures were familiar, yet distant. I was surrounded by people—and yet painfully alone. I was functioning in the valley. Maybe you know that space. Maybe your bones are dry.

The Wake-Up Call of the Valley

The valley wasn't a punishment—it was a wake-up call. God didn't show Ezekiel death to depress him. He showed it to awaken him. Sometimes, the valley is the only place quiet enough for us to hear God clearly.

That was my turning point. I stopped performing. I got quiet. I let God see what I had been hiding, even from myself. I confessed not just my sins, but my weariness. And that's when the wind began to move.

God didn't tell Ezekiel to collect bones or build better systems. He said, "Prophesy to them." Speak. Declare. Believe. Maybe that's your assignment too. Stop analyzing the death.

Start speaking to the bones. Speak to your calling. Speak to your marriage. Speak to your heart. Say it in faith: "Come alive." But don't miss this: When the bones came together, there was still no breath. The structure returned—but life had not.

That's where many churches are today. We've rebuilt the frame. We have buildings, budgets, and bulletins—but no breath. Order without anointing. Form without fire. God told Ezekiel again: "Prophesy to the wind... Come, breath, and breathe on these slain." Only then did they live.

Let the Spirit Breathe Again

You can't fake the breath of God. You can't rehearse revival. The Spirit only inhabits what is surrendered. He doesn't come to entertain. He comes to empower. He responds to hunger. To desperation. To honesty. He comes to valleys where people cry out, "We want to live again."

Maybe your calling is dry, your heart is heavy, and your ministry is hollow. But here is the word of the Lord: "I will cause breath to enter you, and you shall live" (Ezekiel 37:5). **You don't have to stay in the grave.**

The Invitation to Rise

God is calling His Church to stop rehearsing its death. And start declaring its resurrection. We've spent years diagnosing what's wrong. Now it's time to declare what's possible. The Spirit is hovering. The wind is near. And the question still stands: "Can these bones live?"

You don't need the perfect answer. You just need an open heart. Like Ezekiel, simply say, "Lord, You know."

Because the same God who raised a nation from bones

Can raise your church from apathy,

Your heart from numbness,

Your soul from despair.

This is your moment—

Not to perform,

But to breathe again.

Come alive, bones.

Come alive, pastor.

Come alive, weary believer.

The breath of God is coming.

And this is only the beginning.

Section 2: Life in the Spirit

You can't fake the breath of God. You can imitate it for a while by manufacturing excitement or stirring emotion with music and eloquent words. But only the true Spirit of God gives life to dead things. Emotion isn't the mark of being Spirit-filled. Tears can fall without repentance. Goosebumps don't guarantee His presence. It's not measured by how high you jump or how loud you shout—it's revealed by how straight you walk when your feet hit the ground. Life in the Spirit is not a show. It's a surrender.

Stirred or Filled?

Too many believers confuse being Spirit-filled with being emotionally stirred. The Holy Spirit may touch our emotions—He created them— but He doesn't come to entertain. He comes to transform. He doesn't just evoke feelings—He reshapes us into the likeness of Jesus.

I've seen people speak in tongues, cry at the altar, even lay hands on others—yet walk out bitter, bound, or buried in secret sin. That's not transformation. That's not habitation. That's visitation.

Take Yolanda, for example. She was the first to dance in the aisle every Sunday, hands raised, voice lifted—but by Monday, she was anxious, irritable, and spiritually empty. She was chasing the Sunday high with playlists and conferences, but peace always escaped her.

After a heartfelt conversation, I told her, "You don't need more music. You need more surrender. The Holy Spirit doesn't respond to rhythm—He responds to repentance." That moment shifted her walk. Yolanda began to sit quietly in God's presence. She started praying, journaling, and reading the Word. Her worship became rooted. Her joy, sustained. Her faith, deep. That's the difference between being stirred and being transformed.

Fruit vs. Flesh

Paul lays it out clearly in Galatians 5. The works of the flesh are obvious—sexual immorality, jealousy, fits of rage, and divisions. But the fruit of the Spirit is just as clear: love, joy, peace, patience, kindness, goodness, faithfulness, gentleness, and self-control.

Works of the Flesh (Gal. 5:19–21):

- Sexual immorality

- Jealousy, envy

- Fits of rage, division

- Drunkenness, selfish ambition

- Idolatry, impurity

Fruit of the Spirit (Gal. 5:22–23):

- Love

- Joy

- Peace

- Patience, kindness, goodness

- Faithfulness, gentleness, self-control

Flesh produces work, while Spirit produces fruit. Work is exhausting. Fruit is organic. You don't strive to love—you grow in love. You don't fake peace—it flows from the Spirit. Transformation is not performance. It's evidence. And it's impossible apart from surrender.

I remember Alfonso, a former gang member who walked into our church covered in tattoos, shaped by addiction and time behind bars. At first, he sat in the back, arms crossed. But during a quiet time of worship, something in him broke. There was no fanfare, just a whisper from the Spirit. He collapsed to his knees, weeping.

In that moment, he didn't just receive Jesus. He invited the Spirit to remake him. Temptation didn't vanish. But his heart had changed. One day he told me, "I almost cussed someone out, but a voice inside whispered, 'You're not that man anymore.'"

Today, Alfonso runs a business, mentors young men, and raises his son in the Lord. That's not hype. That's fruit.

Gifts and Fruit—Both Matter

In many churches, we chase gifts and neglect fruit. But Scripture calls us to both:

Spiritual Gifts (1 Cor. 12):

- Prophecy, tongues, healing

- Miracles, wisdom, knowledge

- Discerning spirits, Faith, leadership

Fruit of the Spirit (Gal. 5):

- Love, joy, peace, patience

- Kindness, goodness, faithfulness

- Gentleness, self-control

Gifts display God's power. Fruit reveals God's character. A preacher with gifts but no self-control is a hazard. A humble believer without gifts may struggle to serve effectively. But a vessel with both? God can use them for deep, lasting impact.

Paul warned: "If I speak in the tongues of men or of angels, but do not have love, I am only a resounding gong or a clanging cymbal" (1 Corinthians 13:1).

Flesh vs. Spirit

Paul described the Spirit, but he also warned about the flesh. The works of the flesh destroy families and divide churches. But the Spirit rebuilds what the flesh has broken. Want to know what's growing in your life? Check the fruit. Do you see envy, gossip, and anger—or joy, patience, and peace? The Spirit doesn't just empower. He purifies.

Real Signs of the Spirit

We often equate the Spirit's presence with supernatural displays—tongues, healing, and prophecy. While those are real, the truest sign of the Spirit is what happens in private:

- A wife forgives her husband and begins to pray again.

- A teenager deletes the porn app and opens the Bible.

- A pastor preaches for healing, not applause.

- A businessperson tithes in faith, not fear.

- A survivor forgives—not because it's easy, but because they're finally free.

These are the miracles that rarely make a stage, but they move heaven. I think of Esmeralda, a gifted prayer warrior in our church. She could pray with fire, but behind the scenes, she controlled everything. If plans shifted, she snapped. One Sunday, the Spirit convicted her. She stepped down and entered a quiet season of surrender.

Six months later, she returned—not louder, but softer. Her prayers were gentler. Her joy was deeper. Her daughter later told me, "Pastor, I don't know what happened to my mom, but I want it too." That's transformation.

Living in the Breath

To live in the Spirit is to breathe with Him—daily. Not just on Sundays. Not just at altars. In every moment, every conversation, every decision. It's praying, "Holy Spirit, lead me today." It's catching yourself mid-sentence and choosing grace. It's forgiving before they apologize. Serving when no one sees. Obeying when it's hard.

Being Spirit-filled isn't about noise. It's about nature. Not charisma—character. Not emotion—obedience. Not applause—consistency. So, take a breath. Let Him fill you—not with hype, but with holiness. The flesh will always try to perform. But the Spirit invites you to become. And once you've tasted that breath, once you've lived in that fullness—You'll never settle for dry bones again.

Section 3: A New Breath for the Body

The valley didn't stay a valley. That's the part we often miss in Ezekiel's vision. It began with dry bones, but it ended with life. The bones rattled, then they reassembled. Breath entered them. And what once was a scattered grave became an exceedingly great army.

Not through politics. Not through programs. But by the Word and the breath of God. If the Church ever needed that kind of resurrection power, it's now. All around the world, something is stirring. You can hear the spiritual rattling. People are hungry—not for hype or entertainment, but for something real.

They're tired of surface-level religion and emotional roller coasters. They want Jesus. And they're not wrong to want Him. God never called us to live in tombs of tradition. He made us temples of the Holy Spirit.

Prophecy That Breathes Life

When God told Ezekiel to prophesy, He didn't say, "Remind them how they got here." He said: "O dry bones, hear the word of the Lord... I will cause breath to enter you, and you shall live" (Ezekiel 37:4–5). He didn't send a guilt trip. He sent a promise. Too often, our pulpits sound like eulogies instead of resurrection announcements. We diagnose the problem, and we assign blame. But what if we started speaking hope again?

Conviction says, "You can change—God is near."

Condemnation says, "You're done—God is distant."

One heals. The other crushes.

I think of Javier. His life was in ruins—divorce, job loss, shame. "God's done with me," he told me one evening after service. But that night's message wasn't rooted in failure—it was rooted in restoration. It spoke of the breath that revives. And something in Javier broke. He kept showing up. He joined a group and soon found joy again. Within a year, he was leading others through their valleys.

All because someone dared to speak life instead of guilt. The Church must return to that kind of prophetic preaching. Preaching that calls out identity, not just behavior. Preaching looks at the addict and sees an evangelist. Preaching that looks at the broken and says, "You are beloved"—then looks at the lukewarm and whispers, "The fire still burns in you. Let's fan it back to life."

Word and Spirit Together

Notice the sequence in Ezekiel's vision: The bones came together by the Word—but they only came alive when the breath entered. Some churches are heavy on the Word but dry in Spirit. Others are saturated with emotion but shallow in Scripture. But when both operate together—Word as foundation, Spirit as breath—transformation begins.

Gladys showed me this. She came from a background where Scripture had been weaponized. She loved Jesus but feared the Bible. During a series on Romans, we studied grace—not as law, but as love. She cried. "For the first time," she said, "the Bible feels like it's welcoming me."

That's when healing began. Not through information, but through encounter. Scripture, when breathed upon by the Spirit, becomes often mirrors our flaws, but it also opens a window into our future.

From Religion to Relationship

Moving from dry bones to vibrant faith doesn't take a mountaintop moment. It takes honesty and hunger.

First, get honest. Stop pretending. God won't resurrect what you won't admit is dead. Be real about your heart, your prayer life, and your exhaustion. The valley is the place of truth—and that's where breath begins.

Second, make space. We've filled our lives with noise—notifications, demands, and distractions. But the Spirit rarely shouts. He whispers. And you have to clear the room to hear Him. Read slowly. Listen long. Wait with expectation. Let the breath come.

Miguel was a servant in our church—on five teams, always present, and always tired. "I do a lot for God," he told me once, "but I don't feel close to Him."

I said, "Busyness is not breath."

He stepped back—not because he failed, but because he needed to breathe. Months later, he returned and said, "I finally feel like I'm in love with Jesus again." That's the Spirit.

Say Yes to the Breath

Ultimately, you must act on what God says. Too many believers are dry because they keep hearing but never responding. Ezekiel had to speak before the bones moved. Faith activates breath.

> When God prompts you to forgive—say yes.
>
> When He asks you to repent—say yes.
>
> When He calls you to step out—say yes.
>
> The breath comes when we move.

The Church should replace more content with more conscience. We need believers who are sensitive to the Holy Spirit. Disciples who will say, "Yes, Lord," even when it costs them. You want revival? Say yes to grace. Yes to surrender. Yes to letting Him reshape your priorities, your speech, and your walk. That's when the bones rise.

The Body Rises Again

This is how the Church becomes the Body again. Not a lifeless institution—but a breathing, moving people. Walking in power and humility. Filled with gifts and fruit. Rooted in Christ. Awakened by His Spirit.

> The breath is here.
>
> Let it fill your heart.
>
> Let it fill your home.
>
> Let it fill His Church.

Because this Body—His Body—was never meant to stay dead. It was always meant to rise.

Reflection Questions

If you feel dry or disconnected, you're not alone. God still breathes life into dry places.

1. Have you ever walked through a "dry bones" season?

2. Is there a part of your life that feels empty or lifeless right now?

3. What would happen if you invited God to breathe on it?

Remember: God doesn't need your strength—just your surrender.

Part II:

Walking by the Spirit

But I say, walk by the Spirit, and you will not gratify the desires of the flesh
– Galatians 5:16 (ESV)

Chapter 4:

The Gifts and the Walk

Section 1: Discovering the Gifts

The Church was never meant to be a theater. The platform wasn't designed for performance. And the gifts of the Holy Spirit weren't given for applause—they were given for assignment.

But in today's Church culture, we've blurred the line between the sacred and the showy. Stage lights have replaced holy fire. Personality is mistaken for power. Charisma is celebrated more than character. Yet God doesn't pour out His Spirit for entertainment. He gives gifts to equip His people. He sends them to heal the broken, build up the Body, and push back the darkness.

For a long time, I believed that spiritual gifts were only for the "special ones"—those who spoke in tongues loudly, gave dramatic prophecies, or stirred crowds with powerful prayers. They seemed chosen for something greater. And I felt disqualified.

But Paul said it plainly: "To each is given the manifestation of the Spirit for the common good" (1 Corinthians 12:7). Not to some—to *each*. That includes the shy teenager, the single mother, the former addict, and the quiet elder. Each has received gifts if they've received the Spirit. The Holy Spirit is not selective with His generosity.

If Christ lives in you, His Spirit has placed something within you for the good of others.

When the Gifts Become a Show

Still, for every believer who doubts they have a gift, there's another who misuses theirs. Antonio had a sharp prophetic gift. His words were accurate and stirring. People flocked to him at prayer meetings. But over time, the attention became addictive.

He shifted from being a vessel to becoming a brand. The more people praised him, the less he listened for God's voice. Eventually, his words grew vague, and his spirit dry. I warned him gently, "The gift is real, but it's not yours. It's on loan." He didn't heed the warning. Instead, he pulled away from community, and the fruit withered.

The gift didn't fade because God stopped loving him—it faded because Antonio stopped surrendering. Gifts are not trophies for the talented. They're tools for transformation. And they must be carried with humility. Without it, even the most powerful gift can become destructive.

When the Gifts Become a Blessing

Now, contrast Antonio with David. David never stood behind a pulpit. He was quiet and soft-spoken, but filled with discernment. He had a way of looking into someone's eyes and gently speaking truth wrapped in love.

One night, he told a young woman after service, "Your smile hides a deep sadness." She broke down in tears. She had been planning to end her life that weekend. His soft words interrupted her pain. That's the purpose of spiritual gifts—not to impress, but to intervene. To remind people they are *seen* by God. What makes a gift holy is not volume or visibility, but surrender.

Yes, You Have a Gift

I've heard it too many times in counseling: "Pastor, I don't think I have anything to offer." And I always respond: "That comparison is blinding you to your calling."

Ada, a widow in her seventies, doesn't preach or lead. But she has the gift of encouragement. Every week, she writes handwritten notes to people in the church. She prays over each one before sealing the envelope. One man kept her note in his wallet for two years. He had lost his job and was spiraling into depression. The card read: "Provision is coming—don't give up."

Days later, he got hired. He said, "That note kept me from quitting everything." Ada calls herself ordinary. But heaven knows otherwise.

Why So Many Doubt

Why do so many believers struggle to believe they're gifted? Some were taught the gifts ceased after the apostles. Others have been spiritually abused, told they weren't "anointed enough." Some are afraid to try and fail. Others carry wounds from churches that elevated the stage but ignored the soul.

But here's the truth: If the Spirit of God lives in you, He brought His toolbox. He doesn't move in without leaving a deposit. Discovering your gift demands less striving and more listening.

- What burdens your heart?

- What do people thank you for that feels natural to you?

- What ignites your spirit when you do it?

There's often a gift hiding in plain sight. Tristan once told me, "I don't think I have a gift." He didn't preach, didn't sing, and didn't feel "spiritual." But he showed up early, set up chairs, fixed things without being asked, and helped with kids. He did all this with joy.

Then, one day, a missionary asked for help installing a water system overseas. Tristan, a retired plumber, volunteered. Not only did he complete the system, but he trained young men in the village and stayed longer than planned. Even after he left, they continued to call him "Papa Agua." He smiled and said, "I thought I was just good with my hands."

No, Tristan. You were *gifted*. Spirit-filled. Sent by God.

From Hidden to Holy

The Church is filled with hidden gifts—some loud, some quiet; some polished, others raw. But each one matters. Every single believer has been given something that the Body of Christ needs. Gifts may show up in preaching or prophecy, service, generosity, wisdom, or mercy. Some gifts get applause. Many get overlooked. But heaven does not measure by volume or visibility.

The beauty of the Body is that each part is essential. And when we each walk in what we've been given—not to be seen, but to serve—something sacred happens. The Church comes to life.

So, if you've ever felt overlooked, uncertain, or disqualified, hear this: **You are gifted. The Holy Spirit didn't skip you.** He doesn't adopt children and leave them empty-handed. You are not a spiritual orphan. You are a vessel. And there is something in you that God wants to use to bless others.

You don't need to preach like Peter or write like Paul. You just need to say: "Lord, whatever You gave me—I'm ready to use it." And as you walk in step with Him, your gift will make room for you—Not to elevate your name, but to glorify His.

Section 2: Walking Worthy of the Calling

There comes a point in every believer's life when they realize that gifting is not enough. It's one thing to operate in the gifts of the Spirit—it's another to walk in the Spirit. The difference lies in the space between performance and purpose, between charisma and character, between being used by God and being formed by Him.

I've met people who could preach with passion, sing with power, or prophesy with precision. But behind the gifting was a hollow core. Their private lives didn't match their public ministry. They were applauded on the stage, but they struggled to obey once off it. They relied on their gifts but resisted being shaped by the Giver.

Paul wrote in Ephesians 4:1: "I urge you to walk in a manner worthy of the calling to which you have been called." He wasn't demanding perfection—he was calling for alignment. A life not built on hype or hustle, but on surrender. A life where the outer gifts reflect an inner life with God. A walk that reflects the One who called us.

Spirit-Led Means Spirit-Powered

I had to learn this lesson the hard way. There was a season in my life when I was running hard—preaching multiple times a week, counseling families, leading meetings, and handling crises. From the outside, it looked like the church was thriving. But inside, I was exhausted and spiritually dry. I thought if I just prayed harder, worked longer, or sacrificed more, I could keep it all together.

In truth, I wasn't being Spirit-led. I was trying to lead the Spirit. Then, one Saturday, everything came crashing down. I had a funeral to officiate, a sermon to finish, and a counseling session that ran long. I opened my Bible and nothing came. I felt numb. Drained. Disconnected.

I whispered, "Lord, I don't think I can do this today." And I heard Him whisper back, "Good. Now let Me." That moment broke me—but in the best way. I had been trying to carry the weight of ministry in my own strength. But walking worthy doesn't mean pushing harder—it means surrendering sooner. From then on, I started every day with the same prayer: "Holy Spirit, I can't do this alone. Lead me." And He always has.

Daily Surrender: "Not My Will, but Yours"

Even Jesus had to wrestle with surrender in Gethsemane. "Not My will, but Yours be done," He prayed (Luke 22:42). If Jesus, perfect and sinless, needed to submit to the Father's will, how much more must we? The hardest part of walking in the Spirit is not hearing His voice—it's laying down our own. We all have plans. We all have dreams. But Spirit-led living means putting them on the altar and asking, "Lord, is this You, or is this me?"

William and Taina, a young couple in our church, dreamed of planting a church. They had training, passion, and support. Everything looked ready. But when they prayed, they felt a check in their spirit. Though they couldn't explain it, they knew that the timing wasn't right. So, they waited. Months later, William's father fell gravely ill. William became his full-time caregiver, walking with him through his final season of life.

Later, he told me, "If we had pushed ahead, I would've missed that time. I would've planted something out of ambition, not obedience." Sometimes walking worthy doesn't look like progress—it looks like patience.

Building Character: Fruit, Not Just Gifts

Many chase spiritual gifts—healing, prophecy, tongues—but few ask God for fruit. Patience. Kindness. Gentleness. Self-control. Yet in Galatians 5:22–23, Paul lists the fruit of the Spirit—not as flashy signs, but as evidence of maturity. Gifts are given in a moment. Fruit is grown over time. Gifts draw crowds; fruit sustains callings.

Tania had a gift for teaching. She knew Scripture and could explain it with clarity and insight. But behind the scenes, she was struggling. Quick to anger. Controlling. Easily offended. We eventually asked her to step back from leadership. We recognized her gift, but her character wasn't keeping up.

At first, she was hurt. But she listened. She took a season to rest, seek counseling, and submit to healing. When she returned, she was gentler. Humble. More rooted. Her words still carried weight—but now, they were soaked in grace. That's the power of fruit. It brings depth to your gifts, and it gives substance to your ministry. **Gifts may open the door. But character will keep you in the room.**

He's Not Just Using You—He's Shaping You

There have been times when I preached on love and then came home and lost my patience with my family. Other times, I prophesied hope for others while battling discouragement myself.

In those moments, the Spirit didn't condemn me, nor did he shame me. He convicted me; he helped restore me. Because God isn't just interested in what you do for Him. He's committed to who you're becoming with Him. He's not raising up performers. He's raising up sons and daughters. Disciples who reflect Jesus in private and in public. People who forgive quickly, serve quietly, speak truth in love, and walk humbly before God.

You may not always feel gifted. You may not always feel seen. But if you walk with the Spirit—listening, obeying, and surrendering—He will shape you into someone whose life is worthy of the calling you've received.

A Worthy Walk Begins With a Surrendered Step

So, where do you begin? Not with striving, but with surrender. Pray it with me: "Holy Spirit, I can't do this alone. Lead me." That's how the worthy walk begins—one surrendered step at a time. Let Him empower your actions. Let Him grow His fruit in your heart. Let your life speak louder than your sermons. Let your quiet obedience preach louder than your platform ever could. And remember: The calling was never just about what you could do for God. It was always about who you are becoming with Him.

Section 3: A Body, Not a Stage

Somewhere along the way, the Church began to drift. What was once a Spirit-filled Body started to resemble a production. We traded the simplicity of sacred gatherings for stage lights and scripted services. We began measuring success by the size of the crowd rather than the strength of the community. The Church, meant to be a living organism, began to operate like a curated performance.

But God never called His people to be an audience. He called us to be a Body. The platform was never meant to be a pedestal. It was intended to be a pulpit—a place of service, not celebrity. And yet, we have witnessed a generation shaped more by personality than presence. Churches are often built around charisma instead of character. And while the lights shine brightly on the stage, too many in the pews feel invisible.

The Danger of Celebrity Culture

I once visited a church where the lead pastor was considered a local legend. His sermons were powerful. His social media presence was enormous, and people traveled from all over to hear him preach. Cameras captured every angle. The atmosphere buzzed with energy and applause.

But behind the scenes, it was a different story. Staff were burned out. Volunteers felt more like stagehands than ministers. The worship team competed for solos. The congregation didn't even know each other's names. When the pastor experienced a moral failure, the entire structure collapsed—because the church wasn't built on the Body. It was built on a brand. That's the danger of celebrity culture in the Church. It feeds the ego, not the Spirit. It draws fans, not disciples. And when the leader falls, the faith of many falls with him.

I've felt that pull myself. When people begin to celebrate your gift more than your growth, it's easy to start performing instead of serving. But the call is not to build a name—it's to build people. Spotlight fades; substance lasts. And that truth has kept me grounded more times than I can count.

One Body, Many Members

In 1 Corinthians 12, Paul paints a beautiful image of the Church—not as a company or a stage, but as a Body. One Body with many parts that are all different, but all essential. They share the same spirit, the same Lord, and the same purpose. "The eye cannot say to the hand, 'I don't need you,'" Paul writes. Every part is vital. Every person matters. But that's not how many churches operate today.

I think of Sincere, a quiet man who joined our church after being deeply wounded elsewhere. He had served faithfully at his last church but was never truly seen. "I just need to sit and heal," he told me. So, we gave him space. No expectations. No pressure.

Months later, he asked if he could help behind the scenes. Since then, he's become the quiet backbone of our ministry—building teams, fixing equipment, and mentoring young leaders. He doesn't want a stage. He wants to serve. And because of that, our church is stronger. That's what the Body looks like in motion. Not applause, but participation. Not ego, but grace.

The Hidden Joy of Service

We live in a world that celebrates visibility. Influence is currency. Fame is confused with faithfulness. But Jesus taught us something different: "The greatest among you will be your servant" (Matthew 23:11).

Linda understood this. She never preached. She didn't lead worship. But every Sunday, she arrived early. She brewed the coffee, straightened chairs, and greeted every guest with warmth. First-time visitors often said, "I felt at home the moment I walked in."

I asked her once, "How do you keep doing this week after week?" She smiled and said, "Pastor, this is my worship. I may not sing well, but every cup I pour is for Jesus." That's what we've lost in much of the modern church—the sacredness of service. The holiness of hidden things.

The kind of worship that isn't loud but lasts. When we start honoring those who serve in obscurity just as much as those who preach from a stage, we begin to heal what's been broken.

The Church Was Meant to Be a Body

The Church doesn't need more stars. It needs more shoulders—people willing to put down their microphones to carry burdens. The usher with a flashlight may be just as vital as the preacher with a pulpit. The intercessor who prays in private may be holding up the entire church in ways no one sees.

And when we start seeing each other that way—not as competition but as connection—something shifts. Jealousy fades. Ego dies. Love rises. We stop comparing roles and start completing one another. This is how the Church becomes the Body again—not a building, not a brand, but a people bound together in love and purpose.

I think of the early Church in Acts. No stage. No spotlight. Just Spirit-filled believers breaking bread, sharing burdens, and praying in unity. And God added to their number daily. Not because of clever marketing—but because they lived as one.

They weren't consumers; they were contributors. They weren't fans; they were family. And we need to return to that.

Leaving the Stage, Embracing the Cross

If we're going to walk by the Spirit, we must lay down the spirit of performance. The cross, not the spotlight, is our model. Jesus didn't come to be served but to serve. He washed feet. He ate with outcasts. He spent His final hours not in a palace, but on a cross. And He told us to follow Him.

So, we must ask: Are we following Jesus, or are we following personalities? Are we building altars or building platforms? Do we value the unseen members of the Body—or only the ones who make noise? Because the Holy Spirit doesn't just empower preachers. He empowers parents. He anoints hospitality. He blesses administrators, teachers, encouragers, givers, and caretakers.

Every part, every person, and every gift matters.

You Belong in the Body

And that includes you. You're not just meant to sit in a pew. You're more than another face in the crowd. You are a part of the Body of Christ. Maybe you feel like a pinky toe—small, unseen, unimportant.

But even the smallest part plays a vital role. When you don't show up, something is missing. When you don't serve, someone goes unsupported. When you withhold your gift, the Body limps instead of runs.

You matter. Not because of what you produce, but because of who you are: a Spirit-filled, blood-bought member of Christ's Body. So, stop waiting for a spotlight, and start serving where you are. Ask the Spirit to guide you, place you, and use you—not for fame, but for fruit. Because when every part does its work in love, the Church doesn't just grow. It comes alive.

Reflection Questions

You were made to matter. Serving isn't just for the stage—it's for the soul.

1. Do you believe God gave you gifts for a reason?

2. Are you using those gifts to serve others, or are you waiting to be noticed?

3. What's one way you can say "yes" to serving this week?

Remember: Ministry isn't about being seen. It's about being available.

Chapter 5:

Grace, Faith, and the Law We Keep Resurrecting

Section 1: What Is Grace?

I remember the moment grace finally made sense—not just as a sermon or a doctrine, but as a lifeline. The clarity didn't happen during a revival meeting or because of a quote from a book. It came late one night after I had said some things in a meeting that I deeply regretted—defensive, harsh, and un-Christlike. I knew better; I had even preached better. But once again, I had fallen short.

Slumped in my office chair, I whispered, "God, I don't know why You keep putting up with me." And in the silence that followed, I sensed something deep within my spirit: **"Because you're Mine. Not because you're perfect. Not because you've earned it. Because My grace is greater than your failure."** That was the moment grace became more than theology. It became rescue.

Grace Is Not a License—It's a Lifeline

We often treat grace like a theological accessory—something to quote but rarely experience. But grace isn't a loophole, nor is it an excuse to keep sinning. Grace is power. Power to get back up. Power to change. Power to live free. Grace upholds God's standard while lifting us—not through striving, but through surrender.

Some misuse grace to justify compromise: "Nobody's perfect—that's why we have grace." But that mindset misses the miracle. Others fear that too much grace will lead to rebellion, so they cling to rules, trying to control people into holiness.

But here's what I've learned: **Those who truly understand grace don't want to sin more. They want to sin less—not from fear, but from gratitude.** Grace doesn't dismiss the cost of sin—it magnifies the cost Christ paid to forgive it.

The Prodigal Son vs. the Older Brother

One of Jesus' most famous parables paints the clearest contrast between grace and legalism. The younger son rebels, wastes everything, and crawls home expecting judgment. But instead of condemnation, he's met with a robe, a ring, and a celebration. That's grace.

But the older brother? He can't rejoice. "I've never disobeyed," he complains, "and you never threw a party for me." His love was transactional. He obeyed for the reward, not from relationship. That's legalism. Legalism keeps score. It resents mercy. It assumes that obedience entitles us to blessing. It can live in the Father's house and still not know the Father's heart.

I've been that older brother. Maybe you have too—serving faithfully but wondering why someone else received the breakthrough you've been praying for. But grace doesn't reward the deserving. **It restores the broken.** And until we see ourselves as the prodigal, we'll never truly understand grace. Even our best efforts were never enough to make us righteous. Grace doesn't meet us where we're strong. It meets us where we finally admit we're weak.

When Grace Becomes Personal

Blanca came to our church carrying the weight of addiction, broken relationships, and deep shame. She sat in the back row every Sunday, eyes down, often slipping out before the altar call. One day, I caught her on the way out and said, "It's good to see you."

She looked startled. "I don't belong here, Pastor. I've done too much." But grace doesn't judge people's pasts. It listens for repentance. Weeks later, during worship, she broke. At the altar, through tears, she whispered, "I don't know how to be good. I just don't want to be who I was." That's when grace met her. Not when she had it all figured out—but when she admitted she didn't. Today, Blanca leads a recovery group, mentoring young women. She radiates peace. Although she's not perfect, she's free. That's grace. It doesn't demand perfection. It invites surrender. And it transforms from the inside out.

The Grace That Changes Everything

The longer I walk with Jesus, the more I realize how much more I need grace. I don't outgrow it. I grow deeper into it. When I find myself trying to earn God's approval through performance or spiritual striving, I remember that night in my office. I remember the whisper: **"You're Mine. Not because you got it right. Because I chose you."**

Grace isn't just a concept. It's a person. Grace is Jesus, kneeling beside sinners, dining with tax collectors, touching lepers, and defending the guilty. Grace is the cross. Grace is the empty tomb. Grace is the Holy Spirit poured out on imperfect people who fall short but keep getting up. And when you've truly experienced grace, you don't want to sin more. You want to know Jesus more. You don't obey to earn. **You obey because you're loved.**

So, if today you feel like you've failed too much, drifted too far, or disappointed God too deeply, hear this: Grace is not a crutch for the weak. It's not a loophole for the lazy. It's not a reward for the good. It's the breath of God for the dead. It's the embrace of a Father running toward a child still covered in shame. It's the banquet prepared for the soul that never thought it would be invited home.

Law vs. Grace: A Better Covenant

Many believers still live under a mixture of grace and law. They come to Jesus freely but then try to maintain their salvation through rules, forgetting that Jesus didn't come to patch up the old system—He came to replace it. Here's a simple comparison to drive it home:

Old Covenant (Law)	New Covenant (Grace)
Given through Moses (John 1:17)	Given through Jesus Christ (John 1:17)
Written on stone (Exodus 31:18)	Written on hearts (Jer. 31:33; Heb. 8:10)

Old Covenant (Law)	New Covenant (Grace)
Based on works (Deut. 28:1–2)	Based on faith (Eph. 2:8–9)
Conditional blessings	Unconditional love
Reveals sin but cannot remove it (Rom. 3:20)	Cleanses sin through Christ (Heb. 9:14)
Repeated sacrifices	One perfect sacrifice (Heb. 10:12)
Ministry of condemnation (2 Cor. 3:9)	Ministry of righteousness (2 Cor. 3:9)
Keeps distance (veil remains)	Gives access (veil torn – Matt. 27:51)
External rules	Internal transformation
Leads to death (Rom. 7:10)	Leads to life (Rom. 8:2)

The Law was a mirror. It could show your sin, but it couldn't wash it away.

Grace is the water. It cleanses. It renews. It makes you whole.

The cross never represented what we could do for God. It always showed what God did for us.

Section 2: Faith That Pleases God

There are days when faith feels easy because our prayers are answered, our paths are clear, and the presence of God feels near. But the kind of faith that truly pleases God isn't proven in those moments. It's forged in the fire. It rises in the dark—when life hurts, when questions outnumber answers, and when all you can do is hold on.

That's when faith evolves from a feeling into a choice—a rooted decision to trust God, even when everything around you is falling apart. For a long time, I thought faith required confidence—bold declarations, speaking promises, and standing tall in the face of adversity. And yes, there's a place for that. But true faith is deeper. It's not just about being bold. It's about being dependent. Sometimes, it's not standing tall—it's getting out of bed after a night of tears. It's showing up for worship when your heart is broken. It's whispering prayers when God seems silent. It's saying, "I still believe," when nothing makes sense.

Believing Without Seeing

Hebrews 11, often called the "Hall of Faith," opens with this powerful line: "Now faith is the assurance of things hoped for, the conviction of things not seen." That's the tension. Faith isn't proven by what you see—it's measured by who you trust.

- Abel brought a better offering.

- Noah built an ark while the skies were still clear.

- Abraham left home without knowing where he was going.

- Sarah believed for a child after decades of waiting.

- Moses turned his back on a palace to stand with slaves.

Most of them died without seeing the fulfillment of their promises. But still, they believed. That's what pleased God. Not perfection. Not outcomes. **Persistence. Obedience. Faith.**

When Faith Meets Grief

The real test of faith shows up in sorrow. You can preach about trust and sing about hope, but when your heart breaks—when death comes, when prayers go unanswered, when dreams are shattered—your deepest beliefs are revealed.

I remember the night my firstborn son, **Jose Ramón**, died. Just six years old and taken so suddenly by bacterial meningitis. I held his body in my arms—numb, broken, unable to breathe. There were no words—just pain and silence. The kind that shakes your soul.

Years later, my son **Carlos Miguel** was murdered. Forty-four years old. A father. A man with a future. And once again, I stood over a grave, burying another piece of my heart. Both times, I asked, "Why, Lord?" And both times, heaven was quiet.

But here's what I learned: **God didn't give me answers. He gave me Himself.** Faith in those moments didn't look like shouting. It looked like surviving. It was whispering, "Blessed be Your name," through clenched teeth. It was standing when I wanted to collapse. It was trusting God not because I understood—but because I knew Him. **And He stayed.**

Faith Isn't Pretending

Faith doesn't mean faking a smile. It doesn't mean quoting verses when your heart is bleeding. It isn't shown through polished prayers or public performance. **Faith is trusting God when you're not okay.** It's coming to Him anyway—angry, confused, grieving—and saying, "I still believe You're good, even if I don't understand what You're doing."

Hebrews 11:6 puts it plainly: "Without faith it is impossible to please Him." Not hard—**impossible**. Why? Because faith is the only way to approach God. Not through works. Not through knowledge. Not through religious effort. **Just trust.** Not in yourself. Not in your strength. But in the One who gave His life for you.

Faith Anchored in Christ

At Jesus' baptism, the Father declared, "This is My beloved Son, in whom I am well pleased." That same pleasure now covers us—not because of our behavior, but because of our belief. I've met many who are still trying to earn that approval by praying harder, fasting longer, or serving more. And while none of those things are bad, they're not the foundation. **Jesus is.** Faith is the key. Jesus is the door.

And the Father is pleased when we abide in His Son. Our performance doesn't earn his favor; our trust in the One who never failed does. I've learned I don't need to understand everything Jesus does in order to trust Him. **I just need to stay close.** My faith isn't in results. It's in relationship.

When You Still Believe

Faith doesn't erase pain. It doesn't eliminate doubt. But it redefines how we walk through both. Faith says, "I'm not okay—but I'm not letting go." It doesn't mean you never fall. It means when you fall, you fall into grace. It means when you grieve, you grieve with hope. It means when you question, you still trust the One who has never failed.

And that kind of faith—the raw, unfiltered, "I'm still holding on" kind of faith—is what moves God's heart.

> So, if you're still whispering Jesus' name in the dark . . .

> If you're still showing up when it hurts . . .

> If you're still choosing to believe, even when everything says quit . . .

That faith pleases Him.

Not because it's strong. Not because it's loud. But because it's real. Because it's anchored. Because it trusts the One who is faithful—even when we are not. And that kind of faith? **It will carry you through.**

Section 3: Leaving the Law Behind

The hardest part of the Christian journey is staying in grace after we've received it. Most of us come to Jesus the right way: broken, humbled, and aware that we could never earn God's love. We cling to grace like a lifeline, confessing our need and embracing forgiveness. But somewhere along the way, something shifts. We begin measuring ourselves again—by our performance, our progress, and our ability to keep from falling.

Slowly, quietly, we slip back into the very system Jesus freed us from. We start in the Spirit but try to finish in the flesh. Instead of abiding in Christ, we begin striving for Him. We trade dependence for discipline. We replace intimacy with effort. And without realizing it, we start walking with the Pharisees—people who knew the Law but didn't know the Lord.

Christians Who Live Like Pharisees

I remember sitting with a young man named Hector. He was raised in church, faithful to the rules, fluent in Scripture—but exhausted. You could see it in his posture. He looked like someone carrying a backpack full of bricks.

"I do everything I'm supposed to," he said. "I pray. I fast. I tithe. I don't drink. I don't curse. But I feel… nothing. No joy. No peace. Just pressure."

I asked him gently, "When was the last time you were with Jesus—not to earn something, just to be with Him?"

He stared at me for a long moment. "I don't know if I've ever done that."

That conversation stayed with me. Hector loved God, but he was still living under law. Not the Mosaic Law, maybe, but a self-made version that resembled a scoreboard of performance. A checklist of righteousness. A faith that began in grace but became a burden. And he's not the only one.

The Pharisees were the most religious people in Jesus' day. They tithed, fasted, memorized the Scriptures, and kept the law with intense discipline. But when Jesus stood in front of them, full of grace and truth, they couldn't recognize Him. Why?

Because their identity wasn't in God. It was in their ability to follow the rules. And when He offered mercy to those who hadn't "earned it," they saw it as a threat. They couldn't celebrate grace because they didn't think they needed it. But here's the truth: **If we lose grace, we lose Jesus.**

Paul's Letters: A Warning and a Lifeline

That's exactly what Paul fought so passionately against. Over and over, in nearly every letter, he warned the early Church not to return to the law.

> To the Galatians: "You foolish Galatians! Who has bewitched you? After beginning by the Spirit, are you now trying to attain your goal by human effort?" (Gal. 3:1–3)

> To the Colossians: "Why do you submit to rules—'Do not handle! Do not taste! Do not touch!'? These are destined to perish with use, because they are based on human commands and teachings" (Col. 2:20–22).

> To the Romans: "No one will be declared righteous in God's sight by the works of the law; rather, through the law we become conscious of our sin" (Rom. 3:20).

The message was clear: The law could reveal sin, but it could never remove it. Only grace could do that. Paul knew firsthand what it was like to live under the weight of performance. He had been a Pharisee of Pharisees. But when he met Jesus, his scorecard shattered. His status meant nothing. And from that moment on, he made it his mission to proclaim a gospel of grace—not just for salvation, but for sanctification.

Law Divides. Grace Unites.

One of the most dangerous effects of legalism is that it doesn't just damage your walk with God—it damages your relationships with others. Law divides. Grace unites. When you live by rules, you compare. You compete. You judge. You become suspicious of those who don't worship like you, dress like you, or interpret Scripture the same way you do.

But grace? Grace levels the playing field. It reminds us that we were all lost. That we were all saved the same way—by mercy, not merit. Years ago, I joined a prison ministry where volunteers from all backgrounds served together—Catholics, Pentecostals, Baptists, and Charismatics. No one argued theology. We were too busy washing feet, laying hands, and watching God move. Grace had brought us together, and the Spirit had made us one.

That's what grace does. It tears down walls. It builds bridges. It makes room at the table.

Jesus Didn't Die to Modify the Law—He Came to Fulfill It

Some believers still try to mix covenants. They trust Jesus for salvation but cling to rules for righteousness. But Jesus didn't come to patch up the old system. He came to fulfill it—and then replace it with something better.

When He cried out on the cross, "It is finished," He wasn't just talking about His suffering. He was declaring the end of a system. The veil tore. The old covenant passed. And a new way—through faith—was born. We no longer live under a ministry of condemnation. We live under a ministry of righteousness. Not earned, but given.

The cross didn't lower the standard—it met it. And now, instead of being driven by fear, we are drawn by love.

Grace Doesn't Lower the Bar—It Changes the Heart

Some fear that preaching grace will lead to compromise—that if people believe they're forgiven, they'll stop trying to live holy lives. But here's what I've seen: When grace is truly received, it produces more holiness, not less. Because grace cleans the outside, but it also purifies the inside.

When the Holy Spirit seals you, He doesn't just stamp your forehead. He transforms your desires. He convicts you—not to shame you, but to shape you. He leads you away from sin—not because you're afraid of being caught, but because you love the One who saved you.

That's the fruit of grace. It's not passivity. It's power. It's not permission to sin. It's the power to overcome sin.

Come Back to Grace

If you're tired of performing . . .

If you feel like you're never doing enough . . .

If your faith feels like a burden instead of a blessing . . .

Come back. Back to the cross. Back to the grace that found you. Back to the Savior who still whispers, "You're Mine." You don't have to earn what Jesus already gave. You don't have to fix yourself to be loved. You don't have to carry the weight of the law anymore. You were never meant to.

So lay down your spiritual clipboard. Tear up your scorecard. And rest in the finished work of Christ. Because grace is not just the starting point of your faith. **It's the whole journey.**

Reflection Questions

Let go of trying to earn what God has already given.

1. Have you been trying to prove your worth to God or receive His grace?

2. Are there areas where you've judged others by rules more than love?

3. What would it feel like to rest in God's acceptance instead of striving?

Remember: Grace means you don't have to pretend anymore. You just have to come.

Chapter 6:

Prayer, Fasting, and Real Devotion

Section 1: Learning to Pray Again

There was a season in my life when prayer felt more like a task than a desire. I knew how to pray, as I had done it for years. I knew the right words, the expected rhythm, and the spiritual tone. But somewhere in the routine, I lost the wonder. Prayer became a checklist. Predictable. Controlled.

One day, during what I called my "quiet time," I sat down, closed my eyes, opened my mouth—and nothing came out. Just silence. I tried again. Still nothing. For a moment I thought, *What's wrong with me?* But in that silence, I realized something deeper: I hadn't run out of words—I had run out of religion. And God was calling me into something more. That day, I had to learn to pray again.

Jesus' Model Prayer: Not Repetition, but Revelation

I had heard the Lord's Prayer my whole life: "Our Father, who art in heaven..." It was spoken at funerals, recited at services, and etched into plaques. I respected it, but I misunderstood it. I thought it was a sacred script, a polished recitation. But Jesus didn't give us a script— He gave us a structure. He didn't intend its use for ritual, but for revelation. He said, "When you pray, do not heap up empty phrases... Pray then like this" (Matt. 6:7–9). In other words: don't perform. Just be real.

The first time I slowed down and truly meditated on that prayer, I was undone. "Our Father..." Not Judge. Not Taskmaster. Father. That one word changed everything. I had preached on the love of God countless times. But to say "Father" and believe it? That was new. It made me ask: *Do I approach God as a son or as an employee?* Had I been reporting to Him, rather than resting in Him?

Each line of the Lord's Prayer dismantled my performance:

- "Hallowed be Thy name…"—Worship. Shifting from self to His glory.

- "Thy kingdom come…"—Surrender. His will, not mine.

- "Give us this day…"—Trust. One day at a time.

- "Forgive us…"—Humility. I'm not above correction.

- "Lead us not into temptation…"—Dependence. I can't do this alone.

Prayer is not a recital. It's a path to intimacy.

The Prayer That Changed My Life

The shift didn't happen in a revival tent—it happened in my car. After a hard week in ministry, I got behind the wheel, turned off the radio, and sat in silence. No words. No strength. Finally, I whispered, "Father… I'm tired." That was it. No spiritual tone. No King James English. Just honesty. What followed wasn't thunder or visions. It was peace, followed by a quiet awareness of God's presence. I sensed Him saying, "I know. And I'm here." That was the moment prayer became real again. I wasn't a pastor in that moment—I was a son. And the Lord met me, not because I had impressive words but because I came with an open heart.

Since then, my prayers have changed. I pray while walking, driving, and folding laundry. I ask, "What do You think about this?" I say, "Thank You" often. I stopped trying to impress heaven and started talking to my Father.

When Words Won't Come

But what about when the pain runs too deep for words? After my son Carlos died, I sat in my room holding his jacket. I couldn't speak. I couldn't pray. I just wept. And in that silence, the Holy Spirit reminded me of Romans 8:26: "The Spirit helps us in our weakness... with groanings too deep for words."

Prayer, I realized, isn't always verbal. Sometimes it's a sigh. Sometimes it's a tear. God speaks that language fluently. He's not waiting for eloquence. He's waiting for honesty.

Prayer Means Getting Real, Not Getting It Right

So, if your prayer life feels dry or distant—don't give up. Start again. Find a quiet space. Whisper His name. If all you can say is "Help," say it. If you only have tears, offer them. Prayer isn't built on performance. It's rooted in presence. It's not about sounding holy—it's about being whole. Learn to pray again. Not like before. But like Jesus taught us. As a child. As a son. As someone who knows their Father is listening. Because He is. And He always has been.

Section 2: The Discipline of Fasting

Fasting didn't become real to me until one of the darkest seasons of my life. I had fasted before—Daniel fasts, juice fasts, corporate fasts—but most of those felt like routines. I knew the structure. I knew what was expected. But this time was different. I wasn't fasting for tradition or even for a breakthrough. I was fasting because I was desperate to feel God's presence when everything else felt hollow.

One morning, I stood in my kitchen physically hungry, but not just for food. I wanted clarity. I yearned for peace. I needed to know God was still near. So, I began. No announcement. No spiritual plan. Just water, silence, and prayer. And in that place, I felt lighter in both body and soul.

Fasting in Scripture: Focus Over Formula

All throughout Scripture, fasting is a sacred pattern of surrender. Moses fasted before receiving the Law. Esther fasted before confronting the king. Jesus fasted before launching His ministry.

In each case, the fast was not a spiritual performance—it was preparation. It was never intended to earn God's attention but to clear the distractions so they could hear His voice.

Jesus fasted not to impress anyone but to align Himself with the Father's will. He went into the wilderness full of the Spirit and came out in power. That's what fasting does: It doesn't create power—it creates space for God's power to manifest.

Fasting doesn't always involve food. You can fast from media, social distractions, entertainment—anything that clouds your ability to hear from God. I've learned the Spirit will often call us to fast at unexpected times, not just during a scheduled church-wide event. True fasting is Spirit-led, not calendar-driven.

When Fasting Becomes Performance

There was a time when I fasted to be noticed more than to be changed. I didn't say it out loud, but deep down, I hoped someone would admire my sacrifice. I thought spiritual maturity meant pushing your body to the limit in the name of devotion. But Jesus warned us about this mindset: "When you fast, do not look somber as the hypocrites do… they have received their reward" (Matthew 6:16).

That verse convicted me. If your goal is human admiration, that applause is your only reward. God had to ask me something that changed my posture: "If no one knows you're fasting, am I still enough for you?" That question exposed a lot. My motives. My ego. My fear of insignificance. It forced me to stop advertising my hunger and start cultivating it in secret. Once I did, fasting became less about performance and more about presence. I focused less on what I was giving up and more on who I was drawing near to.

Fasting Practically: Simplicity With Purpose

Fasting is both spiritual and physical, so it requires wisdom. If your job is physically demanding or you have medical conditions, fast responsibly. Don't try to prove your devotion with extreme measures. Start small by skipping a meal, setting aside your phone, or turning off the noise. Focus on Him. But don't just remove something—replace it. Fill the space with prayer, Scripture, or worship. When I fast, I schedule moments to sit in silence, to meditate on the Word, or to simply ask God questions and listen.

One evening, while pacing a dark sanctuary during a fast, I heard the Holy Spirit impress something in my spirit that unlocked direction I had sought for months. It didn't come from striving—it came from stillness. Fasting isn't about twisting God's arm. It's about tuning your heart to hear His whisper.

Real People. Real Breakthroughs.

A sister in our church, Yamalis, once fasted during a crisis in her marriage. Instead of trying to fix her husband, she fasted to seek God's peace. Her husband didn't change immediately, but she did. Her heart softened. Her prayers deepened. Her posture shifted. And over time, the transformation in her began to open space for healing in her home.

That's the power of fasting. It doesn't always change your circumstances, but it will always change *you*. Fasting reveals what's hidden beneath the surface. It exposes pride, fear, and control. It deepens dependence on God. And in that space, breakthroughs happen—not because we earned them, but because we finally made room.

From Emergency Ritual to Spiritual Rhythm

I used to fast only when I needed something—healing, a financial breakthrough, or a major decision. But as I matured, I realized fasting wasn't meant to be a spiritual emergency brake. It's meant to be a rhythm of surrender.

Today, I fast regularly—not always for answers, but to keep my spirit in alignment. When life gets loud, fasting turns down the volume. It reminds me I don't live by bread alone, but by every word that proceeds from the mouth of God (Matthew 4:4). Even fasting from social media or unnecessary conversations for a day can help you reconnect. God honors hunger, especially when it's honest.

I often encourage new believers to begin with one meal. Start simple. Don't make it about spiritual performance. Make it about seeking God's face.

Chart: Types of Fasts in Scripture and Their Purpose

Type of Fast	Scripture Reference	Purpose	Modern Application
Absolute Fast	Esther 4:16; Acts 9:9	Emergency dependence	No food or water—short, urgent spiritual focus
Normal Fast	Matthew 4:2; Luke 4:2	Clarity and consecration	Water-only fast for a limited time
Partial Fast	Daniel 10:3	Mourning, simplicity, seeking God	Daniel Fast, skipping meals, media fasting
Corporate Fast	Joel 2:15–16	National repentance, unity	Church or group-led fasting
Private Fast	Matthew 6:16–18	Personal intimacy, humility	Done quietly, Spirit-led, with prayer focus
Fasting for Direction	Acts 13:2–3	Guidance for calling and decisions	Career, ministry, or relationship clarity
Fasting for Freedom	Isaiah 58:6	Breaking chains, spiritual healing	Deliverance from addictions or strongholds

Each of these fasts teaches us something different. But they all share the same core: surrender.

Fasting Is Not About What You Lose—It's About Who You Gain

Fasting clears distractions. It recenters the soul. It's not a hunger strike; it's a holy invitation. You're not trying to earn God's love—you're positioning yourself to receive it more deeply.

And the reward? Not just breakthrough. Not just answered prayer. The reward is *Him*. His voice. His presence. His peace. When you fast with that understanding, even the growl of your stomach becomes worship. Every skipped meal becomes an altar. Every moment of weakness becomes a doorway to His strength.

Section 3: Building a Lifestyle of Devotion

One of the most important truths I've learned is this: Devotion is not something that happens all at once. It isn't forged in a single altar call or emotional experience. It's not a spiritual high that fades with time. Devotion is built like a home—brick by brick, day by day, through every small choice to seek God again.

For years, I thought deep spirituality meant long hours, complex disciplines, or dramatic encounters. But the more I walked with the Lord, the more I saw that real devotion often grows in the quiet and the ordinary. It's not a performance. It's a posture.

The Power of Fifteen Minutes

When I disciple new believers, they often ask the same question: "Where do I start?" The Bible feels overwhelming, and prayer seems intimidating. Worship sounds like something reserved for church musicians. They want to be faithful but don't know how.

I always give them the same challenge I've given for years: start with fifteen minutes a day. Five minutes in the Word, five minutes in prayer, and five minutes in silence or reflection.

The goal isn't checking a box but building a rhythm. In this space, your soul can reconnect with God. I've watched this simple practice change lives. One young man I mentored, Gabriel, was eager to grow but struggled with consistency. I told him, "Start small. Don't try to be a spiritual giant overnight. Just show up." And he did.

The first week was messy. He didn't always understand what he was reading. His mind wandered in prayer. But he kept at it. By the fourth week, something shifted. "I miss it when I don't do it," he told me. That's the shift from discipline to desire. That's how devotion is born.

Different Rhythms, Same Pursuit

Devotion won't look the same for everyone. Some pray best in the morning, others at night. Some walk as they pray, others write. Some sing, others weep. The point isn't the method—it's the **pursuit**.

For me, journaling has been an anchor. I've always struggled with staying focused. But when I began writing down my thoughts, prayers, and Scriptures, I found clarity. My journal became a conversation with God—a place to wrestle, listen, and remember.

Worship also became part of my personal rhythm. Not just on Sunday mornings, but in my car, in my office, and while walking through my neighborhood. One evening during a fast, I softly sang a song I'd known for years. As I sang, God's presence filled the room. I didn't need a choir or a stage. I just needed a willing heart.

What to Do When You Fall Off

Let's be honest: building a lifestyle of devotion is hard. Life gets loud. Kids need your attention. Work drains your energy. You miss one day, then another, and soon guilt creeps in.

I've been there too. I've gone through dry seasons where the Bible sat unopened. Where my prayers were more sighs than sentences. Where worship felt like effort, not encounter. But here's the beauty of grace: **Devotion is not measured by streaks. It is revealed by how often you return.** When you drift, just come back.

You don't have to start with hours. Just whisper His name. Open the Bible again. Sit in stillness. Show up. That's devotion—being present, not perfect. Jesus never scolded the disciples for falling asleep in Gethsemane. He just asked them to *stay with Him.* That's what He asks of us too.

The Fuel of Love, Not Obligation

I used to think spiritual maturity meant strict discipline—wake up at 5 a.m., read five chapters, pray for an hour. There's value in commitment, but if it's driven by fear, it becomes religion. If it's fueled by love, it becomes life.

Discipline is good, but it must flow from delight. These practices— Scripture, prayer, worship—are not chores. They're oxygen. You don't do them to earn God's favor. You do them because you already have it.

I once mentored a young woman who was doing everything right— devotionals, Bible studies, prayer journals—but she was exhausted. "What if," I asked, "you just enjoyed Jesus for a while?"

She looked stunned. "I don't know how."

So, we simplified her rhythm. She took walks and talked to God. She sat with her Bible and a cup of tea, making sure not to rush or analyze, just receive. Weeks later, she said, "I feel like I can breathe again." Devotion isn't formed under pressure. It's grounded in presence.

Jesus Is the Reward

What's the goal of devotion? Not spiritual performance. Not moral superiority. **The goal is Jesus.** To know Him. To become like Him. To be transformed in His presence.

Devotion leads to fruit, yes. It leads to greater wisdom, deeper peace, and stronger faith. But the true reward is the One you encounter in the process. Jesus didn't die to make us religious. He died to bring us near. So whether you're just starting or starting over, begin with what you have. Fifteen minutes. A few honest words. A song. A Scripture. A journal entry. That's enough. God's not grading your performance. He's receiving your heart. And over time, those daily moments will shape you. They'll deepen your roots. They'll become the place where joy returns and faith is renewed.

Devotion Is Not Meant to Be Carried Alone

One final truth: Devotion is personal, but it's never meant to be isolated. Even Jesus—who often withdrew to pray—walked in *community*. The early church fasted together, prayed together, and worshiped together. And so should we.

Don't try to build your spiritual life alone. Find a small group. Ask a friend to check in. Share your rhythms and your struggles. Because when two or three gather, even imperfectly, Christ is in the midst. Devotion becomes sustainable when it's shared.

Reflection Questions

Devotion isn't perfection. It's presence. Start where you are.

1. How would you describe your time with God—thriving, dry, or inconsistent?

2. What keeps you from meeting with God each day?

3. What's one simple way you can begin making space for Him again?

You don't need hours. You just need a heart that's willing.

Chapter 7:

Giving and Supporting What You Believe

Section 1: Jesus and the Apostles Had Support

We often picture Jesus walking the dusty roads of Galilee with nothing but the clothes on His back and the power of God in His hands. And while He didn't carry material wealth, Jesus did not carry out His earthly mission alone. Many people—quiet heroes—gave from their means and helped carry the practical weight of ministry. They gave not because Jesus lacked, but because they believed in His mission.

Ministry has always required more than prayer and passion—it also requires practical support. Jesus embraced that reality. He allowed others to give, not for His comfort, but to invite them into the work of the Kingdom. Giving is not an act of charity—it's discipleship. When we give to what we believe in, we're not just funding a cause; we're investing in God's purposes and declaring, "I'm part of this."

Luke 8:1–3 tells us of Mary Magdalene, Joanna, Susanna, and many others who provided for Jesus and the disciples out of their own resources. These women didn't just follow Jesus—they funded His ministry. Mary Magdalene, who had been delivered from seven demons, gave because she remembered what Jesus had done for her. Supporting the mission went beyond duty—it was an expression of gratitude.

That kind of giving is sacred. It's not transactional—it's personal. It's not about budgets—it's about mission. And Jesus didn't stop them. He allowed them to give; He didn't need it, but He wanted them involved.

It's humbling to realize that the Creator of all allowed others to support Him. He could have provided miraculously every time, but instead, He welcomed partnership. This reveals something deep about God's heart—He desires to work with us. He invites our hands, our resources, and our participation.

I've seen this in the church: A single mom tithes despite limited income. A young couple gives to missions. An elderly man brings his offering every Sunday without fail. Like the widow who gave two small coins in the temple, it's not the amount that matters—it's the faith behind it. Jesus said she gave more than all the rest because she gave out of her need and trust.

Giving doesn't prove our devotion, but it does release our grip on things and allow us to trust God. It shapes our hearts, aligning us with what matters most. Let's not forget that ministry has real costs. Buildings, food, travel, and Bibles all require resources. In Acts 4, believers sold their possessions and shared everything so that no one among them lacked anything. They weren't pressured—they were moved. Their generosity came from a shared vision and deep unity.

I remember when our church supported a missionary couple overseas. Our budget was tight, but the Spirit made it clear: "You are blessed to be a blessing." In faith, we gave. Months later, that couple wrote to say our support arrived just as they were facing eviction. That gift became a lifeline.

I've experienced it personally as well. There were times when giving felt hard, especially when bills were piling up, but I chose to trust God with my first. And He always made a way, sometimes through unexpected work, other times through provision that had no explanation except His grace. But always, He was faithful.

Jesus taught, "Where your treasure is, there your heart will be also" (Matthew 6:21). That's not just a reminder—it's a reality check. Where we invest reveals what we value. So, I ask: What are you building? What are you supporting? We all give to what we love. Subscriptions, clothes, restaurants—we invest in our comfort. But Jesus calls us higher, reminding us to invest in what brings life to others. Give to what advances His Kingdom.

Every dollar, every meal, and every act of service becomes part of something eternal. You may never preach, but when you give to the mission, you are on the mission. You're feeding the hungry, discipling the next generation, and sending the Gospel. You are part of the miracle. So don't underestimate your role. Don't dismiss your gift.

And don't forget—Jesus still uses people like Mary, the early church, and you to carry on the work.

Not because He needs our help—But because He wants our hearts. Giving isn't about parting with money—It's about participating in miracles. And every miracle starts with a heart that says, **"Lord, all I have is Yours. Use it."**

Section 2: Giving With Purpose

When people hear the word "giving" in church, reactions vary. Some lean in with joy. Others tense up with suspicion. That's understandable; after all, too many have been burned by manipulative preaching, half-truths dressed up as doctrine, and ministries that promised blessings in exchange for dollar amounts.

We've all seen it. Slick slogans. Promises of a hundredfold return. A transaction dressed as faith. But that's not what biblical giving is. That's not what Jesus taught. The kind of giving that changes lives—and honors God—isn't driven by pressure or prosperity. It's rooted in **partnership**. It's an **act of worship**, not a wager. It says: "Lord, I believe in what You're doing, and I want to be part of it."

Not Prosperity Gospel—But Kingdom Partnership

Years ago, I sat with a young couple who had recently returned to the Lord after being away for years. They were barely making rent. One day, they asked me, "Do we have to tithe to be blessed?"

I told them, "No—not to be loved by God. That's grace. But if you want to grow with God, trust Him with everything—not to earn blessing, but to walk with Him."

A few weeks later, they began giving faithfully. Their hearts changed. They volunteered, served, and prayed with boldness. Their financial situation improved—not magically, but through renewed priorities and God's provision. Faithful giving doesn't focus on *receiving*. It's the path to *becoming*—becoming more like Jesus, who gave everything, not for applause but for love. Yes, God blesses giving. But not always in money. Sometimes, He provides peace, unity, joy, and rewards that last a lifetime.

Time, Talents, and Treasures: Your Full Offering

In the early days of our church, we had no fancy sanctuary and no big budget—just people hungry for God.

> Keila had a gift for cleaning. She scrubbed floors with joy, humming hymns as she worked. I once told her, "You don't have to do this alone." She smiled and said, "I'm not. He's here with me." That was her offering.

> Jason, a carpenter, helped build our stage after long shifts. "This is my tithe," he said—not for credit, but for the mission.

> Myra trained our youth worship team behind the scenes, praying over each rehearsal. Her gift wasn't just her voice—it was her heart.

Giving is so much more than money. It's your **time**—mentoring and praying. Your **talents**—skills used for the Kingdom. Your **treasures**—the firstfruits, not the leftovers, offered joyfully. And when a church gives like that, revival takes root.

Real Testimonies From Our Church

I've seen miracles, and they didn't come through large checks. They came through faithful, joyful giving.

Iliana, a single mother, gave her last $20 one Sunday. She later said, "I didn't give to get something back. I gave to defeat fear." That same week, a nonprofit stepped in with groceries, rent help, and Christmas gifts. She didn't ask; God saw.

Then there was the time we prayed for a church building. We were meeting in a small, rented space. We called for sacrificial giving. No one gave a tremendous gift, but everyone gave something.

A boy gave his allowance. Within a year, we moved into our building—debt free. Not built on hype. **Built on partnership.**

Giving That Flows From Love

Giving reveals the soul. You can tell me what you love, but your generosity proves it. Real giving doesn't flow from guilt. It flows from **love**. When you love something, you invest in it. When you meet the love of Jesus, you want to give—not to pay Him back, but to say, "Lord, take what I have. It's Yours."

Paul said in 2 Corinthians 9:7: "Each one must give as he has decided in his heart... for God loves a cheerful giver." Cheerful giving means, "I believe in this. I trust You, Lord." God may be calling you deeper—not to give more under pressure, but to give more of yourself. Your time. Your talents. Your yes. Not to earn a seat, but to serve at the table. Because in God's Kingdom, it's not what you keep—It's what you release.

Biblical Models of Giving

Example	Scripture Reference	Theme
Abraham to Melchizedek	Genesis 14:18–20	Gratitude
The Widow's Offering	Mark 12:41–44	Trust
David's Costly Gift	2 Samuel 24:24	Sacrifice
The Early Church	Acts 2 and 4	Unity
Mary Anointing Jesus	John 12:3	Extravagant love
The Macedonians	2 Corinthians 8:1–5	Joyful generosity

God doesn't need our money. He wants our hearts. And "where your treasure is, there your heart will be also" (Matthew 6:21). We do not fund a ministry—We fuel a mission. Not equal amounts, but equal sacrifice. Not obligation, but devotion. We give because Jesus gave first—And we want to reflect Him.

Section 3: When Giving Becomes Worship

Some of the most powerful moments in God's presence don't always come during the preaching or the singing. Sometimes, they happen in silence—when someone quietly walks to the front, drops a folded bill or an envelope into a basket, and returns to their seat with tears in their eyes and trust in their heart.

In those moments, it's not just money being given. It's worship. Giving becomes worship when it's more than a transaction. It becomes trust in action. We often think of worship as music, sermons, or lifted hands. But in Scripture, worship has always been tied to sacrifice. In the Old Testament, worshipers didn't just bring songs—they brought offerings: firstborn lambs, grain, oil, and incense. They gave the best they had, and it was never to buy God's favor. It was to honor His worth.

That truth didn't vanish in the New Testament—it deepened. Jesus called us not just to sing, but to surrender. Not just to lift hands, but to lay down what we love. When we give with a pure heart, we're not funding a religious organization—we're declaring our dependence on God. We're saying, "I trust You more than my paycheck, my plans, or my need to control." That's what turns giving into worship.

Giving as Trust: A Spiritual Act, Not a Financial One

I'll never forget the day Luis, a new believer in our church, gave his first meaningful offering. He had grown up skeptical of churches, especially when it came to money. "They just want your cash," he'd say. He carried that suspicion into his early walk with Christ. But one Sunday, we were studying Abraham and Isaac—the story of surrender. Something clicked. After the service, Luis said, "I think I get it now. Giving isn't about the money. It's about trust."

The next week, he gave—not out of pressure or guilt, but from a new place of freedom. "I don't have much," he told me, "but I don't want fear running my life anymore." That's worship. Size does not matter. Surrender does. Luis didn't give to earn something. He gave because he wanted to trust God more than he trusted money.

Breaking Chains of Greed and Scarcity

What often holds us back from generosity isn't greed—it's fear. The fear of not having enough. The fear of being taken advantage of. The fear that if we let go, there won't be anything left. But in the Kingdom, giving doesn't mean loss. It means freedom.

Years ago, our church felt led to sow into another ministry. At the time, our budget was tight. I hesitated. But the Lord whispered, "You preach faith—now live it." So, we gave. It stretched us, but it also freed us. It reminded us that God is the Provider, not our budget spreadsheets.

Another sister in our church, Cheryl, had grown up in poverty. Scarcity was her default, and giving felt unsafe. But one Sunday, something shifted. During worship, she pulled out her last $42. It wasn't the amount that mattered—it was the surrender. She gave through tears.

That moment marked her. She began giving consistently. Her lifestyle didn't change overnight, but her spirit did. She carried peace. She walked in boldness. She no longer feared the future because she had put it in God's hands. That's what giving does. It breaks chains. It silences fear. It forms faith.

The Joy of Sowing Into Changed Lives

Giving doesn't just transform the giver—it transforms others. Salvador came to us through outreach. He was homeless and addicted. We fed him, ministered to him, and gave him a Bible. Over time, he found Christ, got clean, and became a youth mentor. His life was rebuilt. But Salvador's transformation didn't start with a sermon. It started with people—quiet givers—who gave consistently. Their offerings bought food, shelter, counseling, and time.

They never met Salvador. But they sowed into his redemption. That's what giving does. It multiplies. You may never know who your gift touches. But heaven does.

When You Give, Heaven Rejoices

In Mark 12, Jesus watched a widow drop two small coins into the offering box. Others gave more—but He said she gave the most. Why? Because she gave from her lack, not her surplus. She gave in **faith**, not for praise. Heaven noticed. And heaven still notices today.

When you give with a heart of worship, every dollar becomes a **seed**. Every act of generosity becomes **holy**. Every offering says, "Jesus, You gave everything—this is my yes." So, if giving has felt burdensome or triggering, and if past manipulation or scarcity has robbed your joy, bring it to Jesus.

Let Him heal it. Let Him redeem it. Let Him teach you how to give again. Not from guilt. Not for applause. But from **gratitude**. Because when you give like that, you're not just supporting a mission—you're becoming part of the **miracle**. You're worshiping the God who gave everything for you. You're trusting the One who never runs out. You're sowing into a harvest you may never see—but that will last forever.

Reflection Questions

Giving isn't driven by external pressure—it flows from purpose. It's worship.

1. What comes to mind when you hear the word "giving"?

2. Are you more of a spectator or a partner in God's mission?

3. How can you give today—your time, your talent, or your treasure?

Remember: God doesn't need your gift. He wants your heart behind it.

Part III:

Purpose and Power

We have this treasure in jars of clay, to show that the surpassing power belongs to God and not to us – 2 Corinthians 4:7 (ESV)

Chapter 8:

Sealed for Salvation—The Church God Intended

Section 1: Jesus' Terms for Salvation

Jesus Christ didn't come to establish a religion. He came to restore relationship by ushering in the Kingdom of God and inviting humanity back into fellowship with the Father. His first recorded message was simple and profound: "The time is fulfilled, and the kingdom of God is at hand; repent and believe in the gospel" (Mark 1:15). With that single sentence, He outlined the core terms of salvation: repentance, belief, and surrender.

Contrary to much of what's taught today, Jesus never reduced salvation to a formula or a recited prayer. He didn't say, "Repeat after me." Instead, He invited people to follow Him in a way that cost them everything. The Greek word for repentance, *metanoia*, means a change of mind that leads to a change of direction. It's more than guilt; it's transformation. Like the son in Jesus' parable who first refused but later obeyed (Matt. 21:28–32), repentance is validated by action.

When the rich young ruler approached Jesus seeking eternal life (Mark 10:17–22), Jesus didn't hand him a script. He looked into his heart and challenged the one thing he wouldn't let go. "Sell all you have," Jesus said. It wasn't about money—it was about attachment. Jesus didn't want his wealth. He wanted his surrender.

This is what salvation demands—not religious familiarity, but a new birth. "Unless one is born again," Jesus told Nicodemus, "he cannot see the kingdom of God" (John 3:3). This rebirth—through water and the Spirit—is not symbolic. It's supernatural. It recreates the heart, fills the soul with divine life, and initiates the believer into God's family.

The call to salvation is many things: an invitation to heaven, a call to die to self, and a summons to live a new life in Christ. Jesus made this even clearer in Luke 9:23: "If anyone would come after me, let him deny himself and take up his cross daily and follow me."

True salvation goes beyond spiritual enthusiasm in a moment; it requires daily obedience. It's not just believing with our minds—it's surrendering with our lives.

That's why Jesus gave a sobering warning in Matthew 7:21–23: "Not everyone who says to me, 'Lord, Lord,' will enter the kingdom of heaven." He described people who did great works, cast out demons, and prophesied, all in His name, yet were unknown to Him. Why? Because activity is not the same as intimacy. Relationship, not performance, is what matters.

At first glance, this might sound like a contradiction—repentance is action, yet salvation is relationship. But the truth is this: A transformed life is the evidence of a real relationship. Repentance is not a payment—it's a response. Obedience is not a way to earn God's love—it's a response to the One who already gave everything.

Jesus said, "If you love me, you will keep my commandments" (John 14:15). That's not legalism—it's love in motion. Grace doesn't remove the call to obedience—it enables it. True grace transforms the heart and leads to visible fruit.

We see this clearly in Matthew 25, where Jesus shares parables that expose the difference between genuine and superficial faith. The wise virgins came prepared with oil. The faithful servants invested their talents. The righteous served the hungry, the sick, and the imprisoned. Their readiness, faithfulness, and compassion revealed the kind of relationship they had with the Master. The unprepared, the indifferent, and the self-centered were turned away—not because they lacked good intentions, but because they lacked fruit.

The apostle James put it plainly: "Faith without works is dead" (James 2:26). Paul echoes this in Ephesians 2:10, saying we are "created in Christ Jesus for good works." Works do not save us—but salvation produces works. True faith walks, serves, and endures.

And yet, how many churches today preach a version of grace that bypasses repentance? How many teach salvation without transformation? A Jesus who saves but doesn't sanctify? That is not the gospel Jesus preached.

In John 6, Jesus demanded more than comfort; many, believing His teaching was too difficult, turned away. Only a few remained. Jesus didn't soften His message to keep the crowd. He let them go. Why? Because He wasn't interested in fans—He was calling disciples.

We need that same clarity today. Salvation was never meant to be an emotional moment alone—it is a lifelong journey of surrender. The altar is not the finish line—it's the starting point.

Jesus didn't say, "Admire me." He said, "Follow me." That means laying down our rights, picking up our cross, and dying to our own will every day. That's not popular. That's not easy. But it's the only way.

This is the Church Jesus died to raise—not a crowd, but a covenant people. A remnant who understands the weight of grace. A body of believers who walk in the power of a transformed life.

We need to return to this gospel. Not a cheap imitation that lets us live unchanged, but the true gospel that brings us to our knees and then raises us to walk in newness of life. Because Jesus didn't die to make fans. He died to make followers. And His call still stands today: **Come and die—so you can truly live.**

Section 2: The Apostles and the Seal of the Spirit

When the apostles preached the gospel, they made something radically clear: Salvation wasn't just for the Jews—it was for all who believed. And with that belief came something profound and supernatural: the seal of the Holy Spirit.

Paul writes in Ephesians 1:13–14, "When you heard the word of truth, the gospel of your salvation, and believed in him, you were sealed with the promised Holy Spirit, who is the guarantee of our inheritance."

This seal isn't a metaphor or vague impression—it's divine confirmation. It is both legal and relational. In ancient times, kings used seals to show ownership and authority. In the same way, God marks those who are His with the indwelling presence of the Spirit, declaring, "This one belongs to Me."

This seal does more than affirm identity—it activates intimacy. Paul explains in Romans 8:15–16 that we have received the Spirit of adoption, by whom we cry, "Abba, Father." And the Spirit Himself bears witness with our spirit that we are children of God. That inner witness is not based on emotion—it's based on transformation.

When the Holy Spirit seals a believer, He doesn't just live beside them—He lives within them. He convicts, comforts, corrects, and conforms us to the image of Christ. He doesn't leave us as we were. He brings new desires, deeper conviction, and a hunger for holiness. The Spirit empowers us to obey and walk in the ways of God—not by force, but by internal renewal.

That's why Paul contrasts the works of the flesh with the fruit of the Spirit in Galatians 5. A sealed life cannot keep producing the same old fruit. The works of the flesh—sexual sin, jealousy, fits of anger, drunkenness—cannot remain dominant in someone walking by the Spirit. Instead, the evidence of that sealing shows up in love, joy, peace, patience, kindness, goodness, faithfulness, gentleness, and self-control. These aren't the products of personality—they're the results of surrender.

Paul reinforces this truth in 2 Timothy 2:19 with, "The Lord knows those who are his," and then immediately adds, "Let everyone who names the name of the Lord depart from iniquity." Being sealed by the Spirit isn't a license to live however we please—it's a call to live holy. We've been marked for obedience. The seal brings comfort, but it also brings a commission.

And yet, Paul also warns believers not to grieve the Holy Spirit (Eph. 4:30). Though the Spirit seals us, He remains sensitive to how we live. To grieve Him is to ignore His promptings or persist in sin. This grief doesn't stem from momentary mistakes—it's caused by consistent resistance. Stephen, rebuking the religious leaders in Acts 7:51, declared, "You always resist the Holy Spirit!" That same resistance can happen today if we ignore His voice and harden our hearts.

The early Church understood the seriousness of this relationship. In Acts 5, Ananias and Sapphira brought an offering and lied about it—not to Peter, but to the Spirit.

The judgment that followed wasn't about the size of the gift—it was about deception in the presence of God. When the Spirit seals a community, He expects truth, reverence, and integrity.

The apostles didn't take this seal lightly. For them, it was everything. Paul, once a persecutor of the Church, was radically transformed after encountering Jesus and being filled with the Spirit. His old life didn't simply fade—it was crucified. What emerged was a life fully yielded to the Spirit: sacrificial, enduring, and faithful to the end.

But even Paul saw others who didn't continue in the faith. He mentioned Demas, who once walked with him but eventually abandoned the work "because he loved this present world" (2 Tim. 4:10). This reminds us that while the seal is real, perseverance proves its presence. True sealing is evidenced by lasting transformation.

Being sealed doesn't mean becoming passive. It means we are set apart—for purity, purpose, and power. We're called to walk in step with the Spirit, not just confess Him. That's why Paul urged believers in Galatians 5:25, "If we live by the Spirit, let us also keep in step with the Spirit."

So, how do we know if we're truly sealed? Not by goosebumps. Not by spiritual gifts. Not by church attendance. But by fruit. Do we hunger for righteousness? Do we grieve over sin? Do we submit to God's Word? Do we love what He loves and reject what He hates?

The apostles never preached an easy gospel. They didn't offer guarantees without transformation. They preached the cross. They called people to die to self, live by the Spirit, and endure to the end. That same message must return to the Church today.

Let us walk in a manner worthy of the seal we've received. Let us bear fruit that testifies to the Spirit within us. Let us not grieve the One who lives inside us. Let us endure—not in our own strength, but in His.

Because to be sealed is not just to be claimed. It is to be changed. And the Church God intended is marked by that change.

Section 3: Transformation, Warnings, and the Future Hope

If the seal of the Holy Spirit is real, then it must produce something real. That's the consistent testimony of the New Testament. Salvation is more than a moment—it's a movement of transformation. It begins with grace, is sustained by the Spirit, and ends with glory. But in between, there must be change.

Transformation starts with surrender. Paul writes in Romans 12:1–2, "Present your bodies as a living sacrifice . . . be transformed by the renewing of your mind." He isn't calling us to religious performance but to daily yielding. God does the transforming, but only where there is surrender. This transformation is not external compliance—it's internal conversion. The Spirit rewires our desires, convicts us of sin, and births new patterns of holiness.

Hebrews 12:14 makes the call unmistakable: "Strive for peace with everyone, and for the holiness without which no one will see the Lord." That's not legalism—it's lordship. Holiness doesn't mean perfection. It means being set apart unto God. The Spirit-sealed life moves away from sin and toward sanctification. Not flawlessly, but faithfully.

The New Testament contains such sobering warnings to awaken us gently, without shame. Hebrews 10:26–27 warns that if we continue sinning deliberately after receiving the knowledge of the truth, there "no longer remains a sacrifice for sins, but a fearful expectation of judgment." This isn't addressing occasional failure; it's a warning against willful rebellion. The danger is not in stumbling; it's in refusing to get back up.

Paul echoed this in 1 Corinthians 10, reminding believers that many Israelites experienced miraculous deliverance, yet still died in the wilderness because of idolatry and disobedience: "These things happened to them as examples . . . written down for our instruction." Starting the race is not the same as finishing it. Some ask, "Doesn't the seal of the Spirit guarantee eternal security?" Yes—if you are truly sealed. But the evidence isn't a feeling or a past prayer.

It's perseverance. First John 2:19 reveals the truth: "They went out from us, but they were not of us . . . if they had been of us, they would have continued with us." Continuance confirms calling. Endurance confirms identity.

The apostles never preached a cheap gospel. Dietrich Bonhoeffer called it what it is—"grace without discipleship, grace without the cross." But the real gospel—the one Jesus preached—costs everything. It demands a cross before it promises a crown. In Revelation 2 and 3, Jesus addresses the Church—not outsiders, but believers. And His words are both loving and piercing.

> To Ephesus: "You have abandoned the love you had at first."
>
> To Sardis: "You have the reputation of being alive, but you are dead."
>
> To Laodicea: "Because you are lukewarm, I will spit you out of my mouth."

But in every warning, there is also an invitation: "To the one who conquers . . ." Jesus was—and still is—calling His Bride back to Himself. Not just to sing songs about Him, but to walk closely with Him. Not just to attend church, but to *be* the Church—holy, surrendered, enduring. Scripture makes the contrast clear: God marks those who are His.

> In Ezekiel 9, God commands an angel to mark those who grieve over sin.
>
> In Revelation 7, God seals His servants on their foreheads.
>
> In Revelation 14, the redeemed are described with the name of the Father written on their heads.
>
> And in Revelation 22:4, it says of the saints, "They will see His face, and His name will be on their foreheads."

That's the future of the sealed: not judgment, but joy. Not fear, but fullness. The seal we carry now is the down payment of our coming inheritance. It's the mark of belonging—the proof that we are His.

But Scripture also warns of another mark—the mark of the beast. One mark leads to life. The other leads to destruction. One is born of surrender; the other of compromise. We must choose.

Just as the Israelites were marked by the blood of the lamb in Egypt, we are now marked by the blood of Jesus and sealed by His Spirit. That seal is both a promise and a summons. We are not saved to settle—we are saved to endure, to overcome, and to live holy. The heroes of the faith weren't casual Christians. They were sealed and surrendered.

Paul finished his race not because he was strong, but because the Spirit within him was faithful. "I have fought the good fight, I have finished the race, I have kept the faith" (2 Tim. 4:7). That same Spirit now dwells in us—not to comfort us in complacency, but to compel us toward consecration. The modern Church must return to this clarity. Transformation, not tradition, must be the standard. Not hype, but holiness. Not excitement, but endurance.

To be sealed by the Spirit is not to wear a spiritual badge—it is to bear spiritual fruit. A life marked by repentance, holiness, perseverance, and deep love for Christ. We are sealed for salvation. But we are also sealed for surrender. The seal does not excuse sin; it does, however, empower us to overcome it. Hebrews 10:39 says, "But we are not of those who shrink back and are destroyed, but of those who have faith and preserve their souls." So, let us live sealed. Let us walk in the Spirit. Let us press on in faith and holiness until the day of redemption.

The Church God Intended

God never desired a church in name only. From the beginning, He has been after a people set apart—marked by His Spirit and transformed by His grace. The Church God intended is not built on crowds, charisma, or cultural relevance. It is built on the Cornerstone—Christ Himself. It is led by the Spirit, devoted to the Word, and committed to holy living. It does not preach grace without truth or salvation without surrender. It knows that grace transforms and that holiness is not optional. It is the evidence of a life sealed by God. This Church doesn't ask, "What can I still do and get away with?" It asks, "How can I walk in a way worthy of the One who saved me?"

It doesn't play with sin. It mourns it. It doesn't flirt with the world. It overcomes it. It doesn't seek applause. It seeks obedience. Jesus said, "The one who endures to the end will be saved" (Matt. 24:13). That kind of endurance only comes from abiding in Him. We live holy not to earn salvation, but because we have been saved. Our lives reflect our seal: lives of obedience, humility, repentance, and Spirit-led love.

One day, the marks of this world will fade. But the seal of the Spirit will remain. And it will testify that we were His. So, let's stop settling for religion without transformation. Let's live Spirit-sealed, Spirit-led, and Spirit-filled lives that are bold, pure, and surrendered. Let the Church rise—not in performance, but in power. Let us walk worthy of the seal. **Let us be the Church God intended.**

Reflection Questions

God's salvation isn't earned. It's sealed by the Spirit and lived out by faith.

1. Have you truly surrendered, or have you just agreed with Jesus in theory?

2. Is the Holy Spirit actively leading your life, or is it just a concept you've heard?

3. What fruit in your life points to God's work in you?

Remember: God doesn't want partial faith. He wants your whole heart.

Chapter 9:

Jesus—The Cornerstone and the Call

Section 1: The Head of the Church—Lord Over All

From the opening verses of the New Testament to the final pages of Revelation, Jesus is portrayed as much more than a prophet among many. He is the fulfillment of every promise, the center of God's redemptive plan, and the One to whom all authority in heaven and on Earth has been given (Matthew 28:18). He is the cornerstone—not a decorative stone placed off to the side—and He is Lord over all, not just one lord among others.

Paul writes in Ephesians 5:23 that Christ is "the head of the church, his body, and is himself its Savior." This isn't a poetic metaphor—it's divine order. Just as the head governs and gives life to the body, Christ defines and directs the Church. Without Him, there is no vision, no power, and no identity. The Church cannot survive, let alone fulfill its mission, unless it remains connected to Christ as its true Head.

To say Jesus is the Head means that He sets the agenda, not us. Colossians 1:18 puts it plainly: "He is the head of the body, the church. He is the beginning, the firstborn from the dead, that in everything He might be preeminent." Not in some things, but in everything. Not just in theology but in leadership, in lifestyle, and in worship. Jesus does not share lordship. He is either Lord of all or not Lord at all.

During His earthly ministry, Jesus made no apologies for His authority. In John 14:6, He declared, "I am the way, and the truth, and the life. No one comes to the Father except through me." That statement still offends today because it leaves no room for spiritual compromise. In a world that promotes countless paths to truth, Jesus stands alone as the exclusive way to the Father.

When He said, "Before Abraham was, I AM" (John 8:58), Jesus claimed equality with Yahweh, the eternal God who spoke from the burning bush in Exodus 3:14.

That's why the religious leaders picked up stones. They understood what He was saying: He wasn't just a rabbi or a reformer. He was claiming to be God. And that claim—then as now—demands a response: surrender or rejection.

The apostle John opens his Gospel by declaring, "In the beginning was the Word, and the Word was with God, and the Word was God… And the Word became flesh and dwelt among us" (John 1:1, 14). Jesus is not just the messenger of truth—He is Truth incarnate. Hebrews 1:3 echoes this by describing Jesus as "the radiance of the glory of God and the exact imprint of his nature."

And yet, this Jesus—the I AM, the Creator, the Sustainer—was rejected. Psalm 118:22, quoted by Jesus in Matthew 21:42, says, "The stone that the builders rejected has become the cornerstone." The religious elite rejected Him because He didn't fit their expectations. They wanted a throne, not a cross. A revolution, not a Redeemer. But Jesus did not come to conform to human desires. He came to fulfill the will of the Father.

Jesus doesn't call for admiration. He demands allegiance. In Luke 6:46, He confronts the disconnect between words and actions: "Why do you call me 'Lord, Lord,' and not do what I tell you?" That is the true test of His lordship—obedience. Not emotion. Not attendance. Obedience. We cannot claim Jesus is the Head of the Church while governing it by human preference, popularity, or performance.

To honor Jesus as Lord means that His Word is our highest authority. His Spirit is our source of power. His mission is our top priority. We stop asking, "What works?" and start asking, "What pleases Christ?"

The early Church grasped this. They followed a risen King, not a religious tradition. Stephen, the first martyr, died proclaiming Christ as Lord while being stoned to death (Acts 7). Paul, once the fiercest opponent of Christianity, became its boldest advocate once he saw past tradition and encountered the living Christ. He endured beatings, shipwrecks, and prison because Jesus was worth everything. Colossians 1:16–17 reveals the scope of Christ's authority: "All things were created through Him and for Him. And He is before all things, and in Him all things hold together."

Jesus holds the universe together. He is not just Lord over our Sunday gatherings—He is Lord over galaxies, governments, and generations.

That's why the Church cannot exist for itself. It exists for Jesus. He owns it. He builds it. He sustains it. Revelation 1:5 calls Him "the ruler of the kings of the earth." No pastor, denomination, board, or trend can replace Him. When we reduce the Church to platforms and personalities, we decapitate the body. We deny the Head.

So, what does it mean today to live under His headship? It means returning to the cross—not just as a symbol, but as our standard. We preach repentance, not popularity. We pursue holiness, not hype. We build disciples, not just audiences. We seek faithfulness, not fame.

Jesus is not impressed by church size. He looks for fruit. He said in John 15:8, "By this my Father is glorified, that you bear much fruit and so prove to be my disciples." Are we bearing fruit or simply creating religious activity? Are we making disciples or entertaining crowds? Are we feeding sheep or drawing fans?

The voice of the Head still speaks. The Church must learn to listen again. Jesus said, "My sheep hear my voice, and I know them, and they follow me" (John 10:27). Following Jesus is not a one-time decision—it's a lifelong surrender. A daily yes. A continual submission to His will.

Jesus is Lord—of the Church, of history, and of heaven and earth. The only question is whether we are truly living like it.

Section 2: Gethsemane—The Call to Die to Self

The Garden of Gethsemane is one of the most sacred and revealing moments in all of Scripture. It is not just the setting for Jesus' arrest—it is the battleground where the true victory was first won. Before the scourging, before the trial, and before the nails, there was the garden.

In Gethsemane, Jesus surrendered—not to men, but to the will of the Father. Luke 22:42 captures the trembling, holy resolve of the Son of God: "Father, if you are willing, remove this cup from me. Nevertheless, not my will, but yours, be done."

This was no casual phrase—it was the soul-cry of the Savior, staring into the horror of sin and divine judgment. Jesus wasn't negotiating. He was yielding. The greatest battle He fought wasn't on the cross—it was in the garden. And He won it through surrender.

The struggle wasn't against soldiers or systems. It was internal. Jesus, fully God and fully man, wrestled with the weight of what was to come. He knew the cross would entail physical agony, emotional abandonment, and the spiritual burden of bearing the world's sin. And yet, He chose obedience. That "yes" in the garden became the foundation of our salvation. But Gethsemane was not only Jesus' moment—it is also our model.

Every follower of Christ will face their own Gethsemane. In these seasons, God confronts us with His will, asking us to choose between comfort and calling and between our desires and His purpose. Dying to self is not a one-time act; it's a daily walk. Gethsemane is where the cross first touches the heart.

Jesus' words in Luke 9:23 echo this truth: "If anyone would come after me, let him deny himself and take up his cross daily and follow me." That cross begins with surrender, not pain. In the garden, we lay down our plans, our pride, and our preferences. We whisper, with trembling trust, "Not my will, but Yours."

Yet today's culture doesn't celebrate surrender. We're told to express ourselves, protect our truth, and chase our desires. But the gospel calls us to something deeper: to crucify the flesh, to relinquish control, and to walk a path that is often lonely, painful, and misunderstood. Gethsemane isn't glamorous, but it is glorious because in that place of crushing, intimacy with God is born. Power comes through surrender.

Jesus didn't leave the garden defeated. He left resolved. When the soldiers arrived, He chose to step forward rather than hide. The agony had passed—not because the cross was removed, but because the struggle had been surrendered. Obedience overcame fear; later, that obedience released a redemptive power that would change the world. Throughout church history, Gethsemane has been the hidden place behind every revival and move of God. Before pulpits and platforms, there was prayer.

Before miracles and messages, there was surrender. Missionaries, martyrs, reformers, and revivalists all had their Gethsemane. They met God in the crushing and rose from it with courage.

Paul wrote in Galatians 2:20, "I have been crucified with Christ. It is no longer I who live, but Christ who lives in me." His spiritual authority didn't come from his résumé—it came from his death to self. He gave up everything—status, safety, and comfort—for the sake of knowing Christ and making Him known.

Peter had his own Gethsemane. In the garden, he fell asleep while Jesus prayed. Later that night, he denied the Lord three times. But after the resurrection, Jesus restored him. Peter's self-reliance was broken, and he was filled with the Holy Spirit. Gethsemane had done its work in him. He went on to lead the Church, even to the point of his own martyrdom.

Jesus told the disciples in Luke 22:46, "Why are you sleeping? Rise and pray that you may not enter into temptation." That same word still speaks today. Too many believers are asleep in the garden. We want resurrection without crucifixion, power without pressing, and purpose without process. But there is no Pentecost without Gethsemane. The oil of anointing flows from the place of crushing.

Gethsemane is where our Isaacs are laid down. Where our idols are exposed. Where our control is surrendered. It's not a place of performance—it's a place of honesty. Real prayer. Real tears. Real decisions. It's where we stop pretending and start depending. Where our "yes" to God is not partial, but total.

Hebrews 5:8 reminds us, "Although He was a Son, He learned obedience through what He suffered." Jesus didn't just teach obedience—He lived it, learned it, and embodied it through pain. And so must we.

What is your Gethsemane? Is it a relationship God is asking you to release? A calling you've been afraid to embrace? A fear you've refused to face? A comfort you're reluctant to surrender? We all have a garden to enter and a cross to carry. And we all must choose: self or surrender. The Church must rediscover this message.

We've preached motivation but neglected consecration. We've filled calendars but emptied altars. Gethsemane is a story we admire, but it's also a path we must walk. Without it, we may profess Christ, but we will not carry His cross.

Gethsemane is where revival begins. It's where true power comes—not from charisma, but from crucifixion. It's where leadership is forged—not by applause, but by agony. It's where ministry is birthed—not in visibility, but in vulnerability. So, we pray, like our Lord: **"Not my will, but Yours be done."** Only then can we rise—not in our strength, but in His.

Section 3: Jesus the Lamb—Fulfillment of God's Covenant

From the earliest pages of Scripture, we see a God who initiates covenant. With Noah, He promised never again to destroy the earth by flood. With Abraham, He pledged descendants, land, and blessing. But something extraordinary happened in Genesis 15: God put Abraham into a deep sleep, and then God alone passed through the divided pieces of the sacrifice. This act symbolized that the covenant rested entirely on God's faithfulness, not human ability. It was a divine guarantee that God Himself would uphold both sides of the promise. That foreshadowed Christ.

Jesus didn't just mediate the covenant—He became the covenant. As Paul wrote in 2 Corinthians 1:20, "For all the promises of God find their Yes in Him." Every shadow in the Old Testament, from animal sacrifices to ceremonial laws, pointed to Him. Jesus was not merely the messenger of the covenant—He was its fulfillment, its substance, and its seal. His blood didn't symbolize an agreement; it ratified one.

When John the Baptist saw Jesus, he cried out, "Behold, the Lamb of God, who takes away the sin of the world!" (John 1:29). That was not poetry—it was prophecy fulfilled. Jesus became the true Passover Lamb, whose blood saves us from death. He was the sin offering, the scapegoat, the atonement, and the mercy seat. The rituals of Leviticus and the sacrifices of Israel were always temporary signposts pointing forward.

But Jesus, the spotless Lamb, made a once-for-all offering that would never need repeating. At the Last Supper, Jesus made it unmistakable: "This is my blood of the covenant, poured out for many for the forgiveness of sins" (Matthew 26:28). In that upper room, He inaugurated a new and better covenant—one not written on stone, but on hearts. As foretold in Jeremiah 31:33, this was not reform—it was rebirth.

Where Adam fell and Israel failed, Jesus prevailed. He lived without sin, fulfilled the Law, and offered Himself as the perfect substitute. Isaiah 53 had already described Him: "He was pierced for our transgressions... and by His wounds we are healed." The Lamb would suffer—not because He was weak, but because He was willing. His wounds would open the door to our salvation.

And yet, even as the fulfillment of every prophecy, Jesus was rejected. He was dismissed by the very people who had waited for Him. They wanted a king with a sword, not a Savior with a cross. They expected deliverance from Rome, not redemption from sin. But the cross was not a detour in God's plan—it was the very heart of it. Through crucifixion, Jesus satisfied divine justice and released divine mercy. He took the wrath we deserved so we could receive the grace we could never earn.

This is the gospel: not that we found God, but that He came for us. And He came as a Lamb. But make no mistake—this Lamb is also a Lion. Revelation 5 offers a breathtaking picture. John weeps because no one is found worthy to open the scroll. Then he hears, "Behold, the Lion of the tribe of Judah has conquered." But when he looks, he sees a Lamb, as though slain. Jesus is both the victorious King and the suffering Servant. He came first in humility, and he will return in glory. He is not only the crucified One—He is the reigning One.

Every covenant promise finds its climax in Him. He is the greater Moses, delivering His people from slavery. He is the greater David, ruling with righteousness. He is the eternal High Priest, interceding for His people. He is the Temple rebuilt in three days. He is the veil torn, the Word made flesh, and the glory of God dwelling among us. From Genesis to Revelation, all of Scripture points to Jesus. So, what does this mean for us?

It means salvation is not earned—it is received. Still, that does not make it cheap. It cost the blood of the Son of God. When Jesus cried out, "It is finished," He was not conceding defeat. He was declaring victory. The debt was paid, the covenant was fulfilled, and the veil was torn. The door was opened.

But are we living as covenant people? Do we walk with reverence for the price that was paid? Do we treat the blood of Jesus as sacred, or have we made it common? Hebrews 10:29 warns against trampling the Son of God underfoot and outraging the Spirit of grace. We must never reduce the cross to a symbol or the covenant to a slogan. The blood of Jesus is not a footnote to our faith—it is the foundation.

Covenant living means full devotion. Not legalism. Not striving. But a life shaped by response. When we grasp what Jesus has done, we do not obey to earn love—we obey because we've received it. Grace doesn't lower the standard—it transforms us to walk in it. It doesn't weaken holiness—it empowers it.

We must reject a gospel of convenience that makes Jesus a mascot for our personal, political, or cultural preferences. He is not a brand to be marketed—He is the Son of God. Every knee will bow. Every tongue will confess—not to an image or a denomination, but to a King.

Every time we take communion, we proclaim this covenant. Every time we preach, we declare the power of the blood. Every time we worship, we stand under a banner that says, "Purchased. Redeemed. Sealed."

Jesus is not done. He still intercedes for us. He still shepherds us. He is preparing a place for us. And He will return—not as a suffering Servant, but as a conquering King. When He does, the covenant will be consummated. Revelation 21:3 declares, "Behold, the dwelling place of God is with man." The curse will be broken. The Bride will be ready. The Lamb will be seen face-to-face.

Until that day, we live as covenant people: **Marked by grace. Anchored in truth. Fueled by worship. Transformed by love.**

Let the Church never forget who Jesus is: **The Lamb who became the covenant. The sacrifice who became the Savior. The foundation who became the Cornerstone.** And what He builds—no man can tear down.

Reflection Questions

Jesus is the foundation. Everything else must surrender to Him.

1. Is your faith built on Jesus or something else?

2. When was the last time you said, "Not my will, but Yours be done"?

3. What area of your life needs to come under Christ's authority?

Remember: Following Jesus means letting Him lead, even when it costs you something.

Chapter 10:

The Story God Was Writing All Along

Section 1: The Legacy I Was Given

Some stories begin with peace. Mine began in fire. My calling wasn't shaped in comfort—it was forged in tension, testimony, and torn relationships. What I carry today was handed to me through both glory and grief, through moments soaked in the Spirit and others splintered by division. If I preach with passion, it's because I've lived through pain. If I speak of healing, it's because I've bled. My life in ministry didn't start in seminary. It started in my parents' living room, at the intersection of hunger for God and the reality of human limitation.

It began with my father. A Puerto Rican veteran of the Korean War, he returned home with wounds—some visible, many not. The war had changed him, humbled him, and in its aftermath, God found him. He didn't come back chasing the American dream. He came home searching for something eternal. Somewhere in that search, God lit a fire in him. He didn't have a church-planting strategy. He didn't have resources. But he had a Bible, a burden, and a vision for broken people to encounter Jesus.

Out of that fire, *Iglesia Pentecostal Roca de Salvación* (The Pentecostal Rock of Salvation) was born. It was the opposite of glamorous. There were no cameras, lights, or stages—just a room, a few folding chairs, and a deep conviction that Jesus could save anyone. My father welcomed drug addicts, immigrants, the homeless, and the wounded. He built a ministry on prayer instead of power. He fasted. He wept. He believed. And the people came.

But he didn't build it alone. My mother, strong and spiritually anchored, was his equal in faith and his partner in ministry. She had a passion for the Word and a deep prophetic discernment. While my father drew people in with his compassion, my mother anchored them in doctrine. She led women's ministries, trained young leaders, and opened the Scriptures with an authority few could rival.

Together, they formed a powerful team, with hearts open, knees bent, and hands lifted. Yet as the church grew, so did the strain. Ministry doesn't just build people; it exposes fractures. The very passion that united my parents began to divide them. My father leaned into compassion, sometimes bending rules to reach the hurting. My mother, committed to biblical order, grew more guarded and increasingly protective of structure and spiritual integrity. They both still loved the Lord, but over time, their once-unified vision became two distinct paths.

I remember sitting in a pew one Sunday, listening to my father preach. Just moments before, their voices had echoed from behind the office door. Their disagreement wasn't about trivial things. It was about direction, theology, leadership, and correction. It was the kind of disagreement that cuts deep because it comes from love and conviction colliding.

Eventually, the tension became impossible to ignore. When my father decided it was time to pass the mantle, he didn't form a committee. He didn't hold a congregational vote. He simply placed his hand on my shoulder and said, "This is your work now." It was both a moment of honor and a moment of immense responsibility. In that gesture, he transferred not just authority—but a legacy. And with it came a weight I didn't yet fully understand.

But not everyone supported the decision. My mother, heartbroken and feeling unseen, stepped away. She didn't do it in bitterness, but in obedience to a call she could no longer fulfill in the same space. She planted her own church. And the day she did, my family split.

That decision left lasting wounds. Siblings became distant. Family gatherings grew quiet. Holidays carried tension. Some relatives refused to look me in the eye. Some crossed the street rather than cross paths. I was now leading a church that bore my father's name but carried my family's fracture.

I preached about healing on Sundays while grieving silently in the back room. I offered hope to others while asking God for my own. And yet, I never doubted the call. Sometimes, calling is not birthed in clarity. Sometimes, it's born through contradiction.

My father taught me to believe for the impossible. My mother taught me to discern the Word. One gave me vision. The other gave me precision. One formed my fire. The other formed my foundation.

Both were right. Both were flawed. And both shaped the man I became. I didn't step into leadership with everything figured out. I stepped in carrying a legacy wrapped in glory and grief. And God, in

His mercy, used all of it. He redeemed it. He met me in it. He taught me how to lead—not just by building, but by bleeding. So, to the one reading this who carries a fractured legacy:

> If your spiritual inheritance is both a gift and a wound...

> If you were handed something beautiful but broken...

> If you love your family and yet ache from the fallout...

You are not alone.

I stayed at The Rock of Salvation. But I stayed at a cost. I chose obedience—not to man, but to the call of God. And that obedience has shaped every message I've ever preached. It taught me to love people without controlling them. To build unity without demanding uniformity. To honor the past without being bound by it.

Sometimes, I still hear my mother's voice in the Scriptures I quote. I see my father's legacy in the altar calls I give. I don't carry bitterness—I carry blessing. Even if the story still has unresolved pain, I trust the One who writes the ending.

This is the legacy I was given:

- A praying father with calloused knees.

- A preaching mother with prophetic fire.

- A church that rose out of brokenness.

- A ministry born not from perfection, but from presence.

Not perfect. Not painless. But real. And out of that legacy, my purpose was born.

Section 2: The Struggles I Faced

Before I could carry the legacy passed down to me, I had to walk through a fire of my own making. The road into ministry wasn't clean or easy. It wasn't a staircase I climbed—it was a valley I crawled through. Behind every sermon I preach is a scar. Behind every altar call is a battle. I didn't get here by talent or strategy—I got here by grace.

Growing up, I was caught between two worlds. As a Puerto Rican boy raised in neighborhoods where poverty and prejudice were daily realities, I learned quickly how to survive. At school, I was expected to assimilate. At home, I was expected to preserve. I didn't know how to reconcile those demands. So, I hardened. I wore toughness like armor. Anger became my protector, and pride became my mask.

I fought not because I was fearless, but because I was afraid. Afraid of being overlooked. Afraid of being ordinary. Afraid of becoming what society expected me to be—a statistic, a dropout, a disappointment. Even as the son of pastors, I often felt like the outsider. My parents were respected, but I wrestled with identity and belonging. In the pews, I felt God calling. But in the streets, I felt pressure to perform, survive, and prove I belonged. I split myself into parts: holy on Sundays, hard the rest of the week.

I carried that division into adulthood and into my first marriage. I married young. Too young. Not because I didn't care, but because I didn't yet know how to care well. I thought love would fix what only surrender could heal. I wanted to be a good husband, a good father, and a good man. But I hadn't yet let God deal with the wounds beneath my surface, so instead of healing, I brought harm.

I was unfaithful. I say this not to sensationalize but to confess. I broke my vows. I wounded someone who trusted me. I fathered children—seven beautiful, precious lives—but some were born in the confusion and rebellion of a divided soul. I preached what I wasn't yet living. I wore the title of minister, but I was still a prodigal on the inside.

One night, sitting alone with pictures of my children scattered across the table, the truth broke me. Their eyes stared back—innocent, joyful, expectant—and I wept. Not because I didn't love them, but because I realized how much pain I had brought into their lives. I had given them my presence but not always my peace. I put in effort but didn't always lead by example.

That night, I prayed a broken man's prayer: **"God, if You still want me... if there's anything left... show me."** And He did. I didn't hear an audible voice. But I felt a holy presence descend like a cloud in that room. A weight—not of condemnation, but of conviction—pressed on me. The air was thick with something eternal. I wasn't dreaming. I wasn't emotional. I was encountering the God I had spoken about for years—only this time, I wasn't standing behind a pulpit. I was kneeling in my own mess.

God didn't scold me. He saw me. And He stayed. That encounter broke something inside me. For the first time, I felt fully known—and fully loved. I wasn't excused; I was called. I wasn't ignored; I was invited. Grace didn't remove the consequences, but it gave me a path forward and a way to rebuild.

I began showing up differently. I started fathering my children not out of obligation, but out of overflow. I didn't lead with control—I led with confession. I no longer tried to earn the respect of people. I started walking in the mercy of God. And slowly, I saw the fruit of repentance take root.

Some didn't believe the change. Some still whispered. Some walked away. But others stayed. Others watched. Others returned. And through it all, God kept sending people—one soul at a time—to remind me that my failures weren't fatal and that Ministry is rooted in presence, not perfection. God was present with me, even in the rubble.

I've sat with broken men, not as a judge, but as a brother. I've cried with single mothers, not from pity, but from shared pain. I've preached grace, not as an idea, but as a man who's tasted it. When I speak now, I speak from resurrection—Not because I rose on my own, but because Jesus lifted me. Paul said in 1 Timothy 1:15–16: "Christ Jesus came into the world to save sinners—of whom I am the worst.

But for that very reason I was shown mercy…" That verse is my testimony. I wasn't the best candidate. But I was the most desperate. And sometimes, desperation is the doorway to destiny.

So, to the one reading this who feels disqualified:

> If your past haunts you…

> If your family is fractured…

> If your story feels too broken to be used…

> **Let mine be a witness.**

God still calls the humbled. God still restores the fallen. God still breathes into what looks dead. He is not waiting for perfection. He's waiting for a *yes*. I'm not proud of my failures. But I don't hide them. Because they're part of the story God is telling through me. I'm not who I used to be. And I'm not yet who I will become. But by His grace, I am walking in purpose—one step at a time, one *yes* at a time.

The struggles didn't disqualify me. They prepared me. Not to impress people—But to serve them. Not to be admired—But to be available. And that has made all the difference.

Section 3–A Bride, Not an Empire

Jesus is not returning for an empire. He is coming back for a Bride. That truth alone dismantles much of what we've come to accept as "church." Somewhere along the way, we stopped seeing ourselves as a people being prepared and started behaving like a people trying to take over. We traded the posture of surrender for the posture of conquest. We confused being ambassadors for becoming architects. But the Church was never meant to be a kingdom focused on establishing force; it was meant to be a covenant-keeping Bride.

Jesus said, "My kingdom is not of this world" (John 18:36). But ever since Constantine, many in the Church have acted as if our primary mission is to build God's kingdom here and now, through legislation, dominance, and visibility.

Yet nowhere in the Great Commission does Jesus tell us to seize power. He tells us to go and make disciples. To baptize. To teach obedience. To prepare hearts, not establish governments.

We are not called to conquer nations in His name but to call nations to His name. We are not sent to enforce righteousness through law but to embody righteousness through love. We are not the builders of the Kingdom—we are the Bride awaiting the return of the King.

And yet, much of modern Christianity has bought into the myth that we can bring the Kingdom to earth through our own efforts. We construct platforms, build ministries, chase influence, and organize politically, often in the name of Jesus but without the heart of Jesus. We speak of "taking back the culture" more than we speak of feeding His sheep. We rally to "save America" more than we weep for lost souls. We defend religious liberty more than we deny ourselves, take up our cross, and follow Him.

A Bride doesn't build a throne for her Groom; she prepares herself for His arrival. She doesn't try to rule in His absence. She waits, she watches, and she worships. She makes herself ready. Revelation 19:7 says, "Let us rejoice and exult and give him the glory, for the marriage of the Lamb has come, and his Bride has made herself ready."

This is what it means to be the Church: not an empire of influence, but a people of purity. Not a political machine, but a spiritual family. Not the saviors of the world, but the servants of the One who is. We are here to reflect His love, proclaim His truth, and prepare His people.

That means laying down our swords and picking up our towels. That means rejecting the pride of power and embracing the humility of the cross. That means choosing faithfulness over fame, surrender over strategy, and repentance over relevance.

We are ambassadors, not governors. Witnesses, not warlords. Disciples, not demagogues. Jesus is not returning to endorse the kingdoms we've built. He is coming to establish the Kingdom only He can bring. And He will not share His throne with our idols, nor His Bride with a divided heart. He is coming for a people who have remained faithful—not perfect, but pure in pursuit.

A Church not intoxicated with power but filled with the Spirit. So, the question is not: What are we building for God? The question is: Are we becoming the Bride He's returning for? Because when He returns, He won't be asking about our political platforms or public personas. He'll be looking for those who know His voice, carry His cross, and have kept themselves from the corruption of the world. He'll be looking for a Bride who has made herself ready.

Let us be that Church.

Let us be that Bride.

Even so, come, Lord Jesus.

Reflection Questions

We are not building a kingdom—we are becoming a Bride. Jesus is not calling us to take over the world. He's calling us to prepare for His return.

1. Have you been more focused on building influence than becoming faithful?

2. What does it mean for you to live as part of the Bride, not as a kingdom builder?

3. In what ways has the Church confused empire with obedience?

4. How are you personally preparing for Jesus—not just as King, but as Bridegroom?

The King is coming.

Prepare your heart.

Say yes to the invitation.

Become the Bride He's returning for.

Conclusion:

From Religion to Relationship—

The Invitation Still Stands

This book began with a burden—the weight of watching the Church drift from its true foundation. We've journeyed through history, Scripture, personal pain, and spiritual awakening. We've challenged systems, confronted idols, and exposed the ways religion can mask relationship. But we've also seen the beauty of what Jesus still offers: a Church that is alive, Spirit-filled, holy, and deeply connected to Him as the Cornerstone.

If you've made it this far, it's not by accident. You may have started reading with questions. You may have carried wounds from church hurt, spiritual confusion, or inner rebellion. But something kept you turning the pages. That something was the Spirit of God drawing you back to Jesus—not to a denomination or tradition, but to Himself.

This journey has never been about returning to old forms. Its purpose is to rediscover the Person at the center of it all—Christ crucified, risen, and returning. Jesus doesn't need us to perfect our church programs. He wants our hearts. He's still asking what He asked Peter: "Do you love Me?" (John 21:17). That is where it all begins again.

The road back to relationship requires courage. It demands humility. It may lead you through repentance, through change, through surrender. But on the other side is freedom. On the other side is intimacy with God that no system, no failure, and no wound can steal.

We've seen how the early Church lived—not in palaces, but in prayer. Not in popularity, but in power. Not with programs, but with the presence of God. And we've seen that same Spirit move in our day, through broken vessels, in unexpected places, and among those the religious world often overlooks. The remnant is still alive.

The Church Jesus is building is still standing. And it doesn't need man's permission to thrive—it only needs His presence. Let this be your call to return. To fall in love with Jesus again—not because of rules, but because of grace. Not out of guilt, but because you've heard His voice calling your name.

Where religion demands, relationship invites.

Where religion condemns, relationship restores.

Where religion binds, Jesus sets free.

I wrote this not as a theologian, but as a man who's been through the fire. As someone who's watched the Church fall and rise again. As someone who has tasted both religion and relationship—and chosen Christ.

If your altar has grown cold, rebuild it. If your joy has dried up, return to the well. If you've been pretending, stop. He already knows you—and still wants you. You don't need a title to be called. You don't need a pulpit to preach. You just need a willing heart. There is a Church still worth fighting for.

But it must start in you.

The invitation still stands:

Return to the Cornerstone.

Walk in His Spirit.

Live for His glory.

And be the Church He always intended.

Final Blessing and Prayer

Beloved reader,

You've walked with me through truth, tears, correction, and comfort. Now, I want to leave you with more than words. I speak this blessing over your life, as one who has been broken and restored by the same grace I've written about.

> May the Lord Jesus meet you in your questions, your quiet places, and your moments of wrestling. May He strip away every weight of religion and draw you back into holy relationship.

> May the fire of His Spirit burn again in your heart—not for performance, but for presence.

> May your wounds become altars, and your scars become testimonies.

> May you walk in power, but even more in humility.

> May your private *yes* to God echo louder than any public applause.

> And may you never again confuse church hurt with Christ's heart.

> I pray that you find healing for every place that religion has wounded you and boldness to become the Church He dreamed of when He rose from the grave.

> I pray you fall in love with Jesus again—not as a theory, but as the Living One who still speaks, still calls, and still transforms.

> Let this be more than the end of a book. Let it be the beginning of a new walk.

A real walk. An honest walk. A Spirit-led, cross-shaped, grace-fueled walk—with Christ at the center.

Father, I pray for the one holding this book.

You know them—deeply, completely, and lovingly.

Restore what was broken.

Heal what religion confused.

Revive what has gone cold.

And raise them up—not for platform, but for purpose.

Let them be light in a dark generation.

Let them carry the fire of Your presence wherever they go.

Let them walk in intimacy with You until the day they see You face to face.

In the name of Jesus Christ—**the Cornerstone, the Shepherd, the King—Amen.**

Visual Guides, Doctrinal Foundations, and Discipleship Tools

What Happens After Death—A Biblical Flowchart

Summary:

When a person dies, Scripture teaches a process that continues beyond the grave.

Flow:

Death

> ➤ Soul separates from the body

> ➤ Believers: presence of the Lord

> ➤ Unbelievers: awaiting judgment (Sheol/Hades)

> ➤ Resurrection

> ➤ Final judgment

> ➤ Eternal life or eternal separation

Key Scriptures:

- Luke 23:43

- 1 Thessalonians 4:13–17

- Hebrews 9:27

Old Testament vs. New Testament Understanding of the Afterlife

Aspect	Old Testament View	New Testament Fulfillment
Where souls went	Sheol—both righteous and unrighteous (Job 14:10)	Paradise or Hades (Luke 16:22-23)
Righteous compartment	"Abraham's Bosom" (Luke 16:22)	Presence of the Lord (2 Cor. 5:8)
Unrighteous compartment	Torment in Sheol (Psalm 9:17)	Hades, awaiting judgment (Luke 16:23; Rev. 20:13)
Access to God	Separated—veil remained (Hebrews 9:8)	Direct access through Christ (Hebrews 10:19-20)
Final judgment	Foreshadowed (Daniel 12:2)	Described fully (Rev. 20:11-15)

Aspect	Old Testament View	New Testament Fulfillment
Eternal destination	Unclear or veiled (Eccl. 3:21)	Heaven or Hell clearly revealed (John 14:2–3; Matt. 25:46)

LIFE, DEATH, AND THE AFTERLIFE

LIFE ON EARTH
Time to choose God, follow Christ, and live by faith

↓

DEATH (SLEEP)
The body dies; spirit returns to God; waiting period begins

PARADISE
Believers rest *in Paradise* (Abraham's side)

HADES
Unbelievers suffer in Hades

↓

RESURRECTION
Jesus returns; all are raised— some to eternal life, others to judgment

↓

FINAL JUDGMENT
Everyone stands before God to be judged

LAKE OF FIRE
Unbelievers cast into Lake of Fire

Spiritual Gifts Reference Guide

(See 1 Corinthians 12)

- Word of Wisdom

- Word of Knowledge

- Faith

- Gifts of Healing

- Working of Miracles

- Prophecy

- Discerning of Spirits

- Speaking in Tongues

- Interpretation of Tongues

Two Kingdoms: A Tree Diagram Metaphor

Kingdom of God

- Rooted in: Love

- Branches of: Righteousness

- Fruit of: The Spirit (Galatians 5:22–23)

Kingdom of Satan

- Rooted in: Pride

- Branches of: Rebellion

- Fruit of: The Flesh (Galatians 5:19–21)

Key Scriptures:

- Matthew 7:16–20

- John 15:1–8

- Galatians 5:19–23

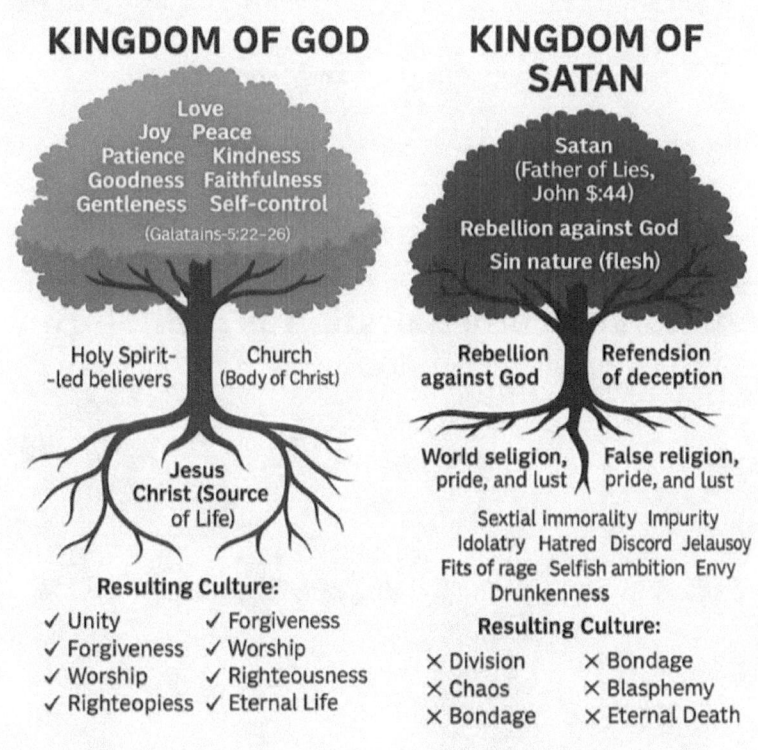

Practical Tips for Daily Devotion

15-Minute Devotion Plan:

- 5 minutes in the Word

- 5 minutes in prayer

- 5 minutes in reflection

Daily Encouragements:

- Create a sacred space to meet with God

- Keep a journal for prayers, confessions, and answered requests

- Talk to God throughout your day—keep it simple

- Be consistent—not perfect

Foundational Truth: Salvation Is a Gift—But Fruit Is the Evidence

Ephesians 2:8–9

"We are saved by grace through faith... not by works."

But...

Ephesians 2:10

"We are created for good works, prepared in advance by God."

Salvation isn't earned—but it transforms. True salvation bears fruit.

Key Doctrinal Questions Answered

1. What Is True Repentance?

- Greek: *Metanoia*—a change of mind that leads to a change in direction.

- Not just feeling bad—true repentance surrenders to Jesus.

Scripture:

Luke 13:3: "Unless you repent, you will all likewise perish."

The question that remains is: Did someone believe and repent, or did they just agree emotionally and continue in rebellion?

---

2. Can Someone Lose Their Salvation (Seal)?

Scriptural examples of falling away or false conversion:

King Saul	Spirit departed due to disobedience	1 Samuel 16:14
Judas Iscariot	Walked with Jesus but betrayed Him	John 17:12 (son of perdition)
1 Cor. 5 Man	Given over to Satan for the destruction of the flesh	1 Corinthians 5:5

Hebrews Warning	"If we go on sinning deliberately..."	Hebrews 10:26-29
Matthew 7:21-23	"I never knew you"— relationship	Matthew 7:21-23
Galatians 5	Those who live by the flesh will not inherit the Kingdom	Gal. 5:19-21
King Saul	Spirit departed due to disobedience	1 Samuel 16:14

3. Once Saved, Always Saved? Or Truly Saved, Always Transformed?

- Romans 7: The struggle with sin

- Romans 8: Life in the Spirit

- 1 John 2:19: Some left because they were never truly of us

True believers repent, persevere, and grow—even when they stumble.

4. Jesus' Parables on Salvation & Fruit

Sower: Only one soil produced lasting fruit (Mark 4:3–20)

Wheat and Tares: Judgment separates the true from the false (Matt. 13)

No Fruit = Cut Off: Even if in the vine, fruitless branches are removed (John 15:2, 6)

---

5. The Sealing of the Spirit

- Yes, it's permanent for the truly born again (Eph. 1:13-14).

- But not all who claim Christ are truly sealed (Rom. 8:9: "Anyone who does not have the Spirit of Christ does not belong to Him").

---

6. What Proves Salvation?

Genuine Salvation Produces	False Conversion Shows
Ongoing repentance	Continued willful sin
Desire for God's Word	Fleshly cravings dominate
Spiritual fruit (Gal. 5:22-23)	No change, no fruit
Brokenness over sin	Justification of sin
Relationship with Jesus	Religion without intimacy

---

7. Transformation Is the Standard

- Romans 12:1–2: Be transformed by the renewing of your mind.

- 2 Corinthians 5:17: If anyone is in Christ, they are a new creation.

We are sealed as long as we remain surrendered. It doesn't require perfection, but direction.

We don't earn salvation—we walk in it with reverence.

Philippians 2:12–13: "Work out your salvation with fear and trembling, for it is God who works in you."

Appendix II:

Scriptures for Meditation and Action Steps

Go deeper in your journey of faith.

Whether you're meeting Jesus for the first time or seeking to grow in spiritual maturity, these verses and practices are designed to strengthen your daily walk.

Chapter 1: From Religion to Relationship

Scriptures for Meditation

- Matthew 15:8–9

- John 4:23–24

- Revelation 3:20

- 2 Timothy 3:5

- Isaiah 29:13

- Colossians 2:8

- Ephesians 2:19–22

- Acts 2:42–47

Action Steps

- Lay down lifeless habits

- Read the Gospels relationally

- Pray honestly

- Simplify your worship

- Be the Church

- Journal your journey

- Invite the Spirit's help

Chapter 2: The Traits and Trials of Leadership

Scriptures for Meditation

- Luke 6:12–16

- Acts 4:13

- Mark 10:42–45

- 1 Peter 5:2–3

- Ezekiel 34:1–10

- John 17:20–23

- Ephesians 4:1–6

- James 3:13–18

Action Steps

- Study the Twelve

- Serve in silence

- Lead with integrity

- Pursue reconciliation

- Intercede for leaders

- Promote unity

- Ask God to heal

Chapter 3: Breath and Bones

Scriptures for Meditation

- Ezekiel 37:1–14

- Galatians 5:16–25

- Romans 8:1–2, 11

- John 6:63

- 2 Timothy 3:16–17

- Psalm 51:10–12

- Isaiah 61:1–3

Action Steps

- Name your valley

- Be honest

- Speak life

- Make space

- Act in faith

- Rejoin the body

- Pray for breath

Chapter 4: Serving With Purpose

Scriptures for Meditation

- 1 Corinthians 12:4–27

- Romans 12:3–8

- 1 Peter 4:10–11

- Ephesians 4:1–3

- Galatians 5:22–25

- John 13:3–17

- Mark 10:43–45

- Philippians 2:3–5

- Colossians 3:23–24

Action Steps

- Pray for clarity

- Serve in secret

- Celebrate the hidden

- Focus on one fruit

- Find a place to serve

- Examine your motives

- Start with the Spirit

Chapter 5: Grace Over Law

Scriptures for Meditation

- Galatians 2:21

- Matthew 9:13 / Hosea 6:6

- Galatians 3:3

- Galatians 5:1

- Colossians 2:20–23

- Romans 3:20–24

- Luke 15

- John 1:17

Action Steps

- Sit without striving

- Identify a legalistic habit

- Extend grace

- Fast from performance

- Memorize Galatians 2:21

- Host a grace talk

- Journal the question

Chapter 6: A Lifestyle of Devotion

Scriptures for Meditation

- John 15:4–5

- Luke 10:41–42

- Psalm 1:2–3

- James 4:8

- Psalm 27:4

- Matthew 6:6

- Romans 12:1

- 1 Thessalonians 5:17

- 1 John 5:3

- Psalm 62:8

Action Steps

- Start a 15-minute rhythm

- Create a devotion space

- Build a worship habit

- Keep a devotional journal

- Memorize one verse a week

- Use prayer prompts

- Reset without shame

Chapter 7: Giving and Supporting What You Believe

Scriptures for Meditation

- Luke 8:1–3

- Acts 4:32–35

- Mark 12:41–44

- 2 Corinthians 9:6–8

- Matthew 6:21

- Genesis 22:1–14

- Hebrews 13:16

Action Steps

- Evaluate your giving

- Reframe giving as worship

- Give in a new way

- Share a testimony

- Create a giving plan (time, talent, treasure)

Chapter 8: Sealed for Salvation

Scriptures for Meditation

- Mark 1:15

- John 3:3, 5

- Luke 9:23

- Matthew 7:21–23

- Ephesians 1:13–14

- Romans 8:15–16

- 2 Timothy 2:19

- Galatians 5:19–23

- Hebrews 10:26–29

- Revelation 7:3–4; 14:1; 22:4

Action Steps

- Revisit your foundation

- Let the Spirit search you

- Return to daily obedience

- Grow spiritual fruit

- Strengthen others

- Speak against cultural Christianity

- Walk with confidence

Chapter 9: Jesus—The Cornerstone and the Call

Scriptures for Meditation

- Colossians 1:18

- John 14:6

- Luke 22:42

- Galatians 2:20

- Isaiah 53

- John 1:29

- Matthew 26:28

- Hebrews 10:29

- Revelation 5

- Revelation 21

Action Steps

- Renew your surrender

- Take communion with reverence

- Live as one sealed

- Repent of misplaced authority

- Study deeply (Isaiah 53, John 17)

- Share boldly

- Confront false gospels

Chapter 10: From Pain to Purpose / A Bride, Not an Empire

Scriptures for Meditation

- Romans 11:29

- 2 Corinthians 12:9

- Isaiah 61:3

- Ezekiel 37:5

- John 21:15–17

- Revelation 19:7

- John 18:36

- 2 Corinthians 11:2

- Ephesians 5:25–27

- Matthew 28:19–20

Action Steps

- Write your testimony

- Reach out to the hurting

- Pray a prayer of surrender

- Take one step forward toward your calling

- Repent of kingdom-building motives

- Recenter your mission on discipleship

- Fast and pray for readiness

- Pursue holiness over performance

- Embrace your identity as the Bride, not the builder

Acknowledgments

First and foremost, I give thanks to my Lord and Savior, Jesus Christ. He breathed life into these pages and walked with me through every valley and mountain on this journey. Without His grace, I would have no story to tell.

To my children—Tania, Javier, David, Iliana, Jason, and Keila—thank you for being my strength and my reason. You have endured more than many will ever know, and your quiet resilience has been a light in the darkest seasons of my life. Your love, even in silence, has spoken louder than words.

To my granddaughter Yamalis, thank you for your tenderness, your strength, and the joy you've brought into our family. Watching you grow into motherhood has filled me with renewed hope for the future.

To my beloved wife, Cheryl Marie—thank you for your unwavering love, patient spirit, and deep faith. You have stood beside me through seasons of sorrow and celebration. Your quiet strength and faithful prayers have anchored me in both life and ministry.

To my co-pastor, Hector Matias—thank you for walking this road of ministry with me. Your friendship, integrity, and devotion to God's people have been a gift. And to Minister Yolanda Rosado—your humility, steadfastness, and servant's heart have inspired many, including me. I'm grateful for your faith, wisdom, and unwavering support.

To Rev. Aaron Payson—thank you for stepping in to conduct my son's funeral and wake when grief rendered me unable. You carried me when I could not stand. You will always have a sacred place in my heart.

To Jenny Pacillo—thank you for your care, insight, and patience in shaping this manuscript. You honored the message while helping bring clarity and structure to my words. Your editorial guidance never dimmed the soul of this work, and I am truly grateful.

To the Rock of Salvation Church family—you are living proof that dry bones can rise again. Thank you for believing in the vision God placed on my heart. Your prayers, encouragement, and love have helped carry this message into the world.

And finally, to every reader—thank you. If you've journeyed with me to this final page, I now consider you a part of my story. I pray these words lead you from religion to relationship, from tradition to truth, and from brokenness into the fullness of life in Christ.

He alone is the Author of this testimony—and the One who walked beside me, every step of the way.

About the Author

Jose R. Perez is the Pastor of **Rock of Salvation Church** in Worcester, Massachusetts—the first Hispanic evangelical church in New England, founded by his parents. Born in Puerto Rico and raised between two cultures, Pastor Perez's life is a living testimony of transformation: from addiction, grief, and family division to restoration, vision, and Spirit-led leadership.

He has served his community in multiple roles—pastor, union organizer, nonprofit director, and mentor—always with a heart for justice, healing, and spiritual renewal. Revival, reconciliation, and a commitment to the unadulterated truth of Scripture, untainted by religious distortion and cultural compromise, characterize his ministry.

Pastor Perez carries forward the legacy of his father, Rev. Jose Perez, who laid the foundation of faith and entrusted him with the mantle of leadership. Today, he continues to preach a message of hope, repentance, and awakening to a generation seeking more than tradition—they are searching for truth.

In *"From Religion to Relationship: Finding Jesus in a Divided Church,"* Pastor Perez invites readers into a deeper, more authentic walk with Christ, one marked not by legalism or performance, but by grace, surrender, and the power of the Holy Spirit. He writes for the wounded, the weary, and those who are ready to rise again.

Visit: www.pastorjoseperez.com

Contact: info@pastorjoseperez.com | books@pastorjoseperez.com

If this book has blessed, encouraged, or challenged you in your walk with Jesus, please leave an online review; Pastor Jose would be honored. Your words can also help others find healing and hope.

www.ingramcontent.com/pod-product-compliance
Lightning Source LLC
Chambersburg PA
CBHW031531120626
46545CB00005B/2100